TABLE OF CONTENTS

Top 20 Test Taking Tips 4
Supply Chain Introduction 5
Basics of Supply Chain Management 13
Practice Test 91
    Practice questions 91
    Answers and explanations 100
Secret Key #1 – Time is Your Greatest Enemy 109
Secret Key #2 – Guessing is not Guesswork 110
    Monkeys Take the CPIM Supply Chain 110
    Success Strategy #2 111
Secret Key #3 – Practice Smarter, Not Harder 113
    Success Strategy 113
Secret Key #4 – Prepare, Don't Procrastinate 114
Secret Key #5 – Test Yourself 115
    Success Strategy #5 115
General Strategies 117
Special Report: What Your Test Score Will Tell You About Your IQ 126
Special Report: Retaking the Test: What Are Your Chances at Improving Your Score?
.... 129
Special Report: Key Supply Chain Definitions 132
Special Report: Additional Bonus Material 165

Copyright © Mometrix Media. You have been licensed one copy of this document for personal use only.
Any other reproduction or redistribution is strictly prohibited. All rights reserved.

Top 20 Test Taking Tips

1. Carefully follow all the test registration procedures
2. Know the test directions, duration, topics, question types, how many questions
3. Setup a flexible study schedule at least 3-4 weeks before test day
4. Study during the time of day you are most alert, relaxed, and stress free
5. Maximize your learning style; visual learner use visual study aids, auditory learner use auditory study aids
6. Focus on your weakest knowledge base
7. Find a study partner to review with and help clarify questions
8. Practice, practice, practice
9. Get a good night's sleep; don't try to cram the night before the test
10. Eat a well balanced meal
11. Know the exact physical location of the testing site; drive the route to the site prior to test day
12. Bring a set of ear plugs; the testing center could be noisy
13. Wear comfortable, loose fitting, layered clothing to the testing center; prepare for it to be either cold or hot during the test
14. Bring at least 2 current forms of ID to the testing center
15. Arrive to the test early; be prepared to wait and be patient
16. Eliminate the obviously wrong answer choices, then guess the first remaining choice
17. Pace yourself; don't rush, but keep working and move on if you get stuck
18. Maintain a positive attitude even if the test is going poorly
19. Keep your first answer unless you are positive it is wrong
20. Check your work, don't make a careless mistake

Supply Chain Introduction

Why Certify?

CPIM Supply Chain Certification can:
- Raise the standards in your field and distinguish your experience
- Enable you to use credentials to further your career
- Improve your skills and abilities to manage workers

First, we must ask ourselves, where is the profit in the supply chain? This sounds like a simple question, but the answer is more complex than you might think. The supply chain has traditionally been presented as a sequential set of functions: plan, source, make, deliver, customer, return, and their many sub-systems and parts. We are used to ideas and systems presented in sequence because we learned both numbers and the alphabet this way by rote, as children. As a consequence, we tend to think sequentially. Unfortunately the world is both sequential and very much non-sequential. The supply chain world, in particular, exists in the context of a multitude of simultaneous events.

Take, for example, the supply chain elements of plan, source, make, deliver and customer, which exist all at once. They also exist in multiples at a time. Planning goes on constantly, and sourcing goes on both constantly and in multiples. A number of these elements may be de-coupled in some firms, such as computer makers who outsource their manufacturing. Outsourcing means not only planning internally, in multiple time frames and with multiple products, but it also takes into account planning alongside a whole other enterprise.

If we look at the supply chain as a non-sequential "profit net" we might see an enterprise negotiating the lowest cost, the fastest processing, and the highest quality in a dynamic context of time, place, and event. If each purchase or movement of goods is thought of as a node in a network, then negotiations can exist between nodes or groups of nodes all along the profit net regardless of mode (source, make, deliver). In fact, what we might see is a series of profit nets clustered around either products or functions - or both. When collaboration between enterprises is involved, a profit net might give birth to collective insurance or a buy into insurance for profit. The collaborating parties might share the risk of supply chain business just as insurance generally shares the risk.

Let's look at the traditional breakdown of "make" as:
- process make-to-stock,
- process make-to-order and discrete make-to-order,
- make-to-stock, and
- engineer-to-order.

Each process is a world unto itself. The planning and negotiations around the events of a make-to-stock and a make-to-order are fundamentally different. Within a profit net context, entirely different negotiations take place simultaneously all along the supply chain. These simultaneous processes allow for added profit value to come from sources not normally tapped.

Make-to-order normally means limited parts (usually of high value) and make-to-stock normally means a great many parts (often of lower value). That does not mean some commonality can't exist. The make-to-order may well be a negotiation between profit net nodes that reach into the make-to-stock process. The profit net can operate within a combination of databases and spreadsheets, making searches intelligently relational and changes automatic. In this context, a manager could virtually play for profit before deciding which negotiations deliver the magic profit number in regard to lowest cost, fastest processing, and highest quality.

Safety stock is needed where uncertainty exists whether the uncertainty is in supply or demand. Uncertainty of supply is generally more controllable and, being further down in the supply chain, it is easier to recover from minor problems.

Safety stock to cover uncertainty of supply should therefore be kept to a minimum and the cause of the uncertainty tackled. Uncertainty of demand is generally less controllable. The stock you need to carry depends on whether the product is engineered to order, made to order or shipped from stock.

For engineer to order companies, design time has to be included. Balanced against the commercial requirement to hold stock is the financial requirement to carry as little stock as possible. If your cumulative lead time is inside the lead time required by your customer, the only reason to stock is to make in larger batches than your customers need or to smooth out peaks of demand.

For companies that would like to be able to ship from stock, you have to carry some safety stock. How much stock you carry in this case depends on your ability to forecast. With a perfect forecast, you make just what you need, when you need it. Every company has to forecast. If there is no formal forecast, purchasing people forecast what to buy, planners forecast what they need to get made, manufacturing people forecast capacity requirements, accountants forecast cash flow, salesmen have targets and so on. Without a formal forecasting process integrated into the planning system, all these forecasts will be different so inventory will be out of balance and you can only ship to the lowest forecast for each product. The solution is to have one agreed forecast that everyone works to, preferably produced by sales/marketing.

Once you have an agreed forecast, the safety stock level for items you want to deliver from stock is determined by the accuracy of the forecast compared to replenishment time. There have been attempts at a mathematical formula for stock levels but in practice you fix a stock level that balances the commercial risk of running out of stock against the cost of holding stock and try to reduce your lead times and batch sizes and improve your forecast accuracy faster than pressure from your customers (and finance)!

Definition

A supply chain is the stream of processes of moving goods from the customer order through the raw materials stage, supply, production, and distribution of products to the customer. All organizations have supply chains of varying degrees, depending upon the size of the organization and the type of product manufactured. These networks obtain supplies and components, change these materials into finished products and then distribute them to the customer.

Managing the chain of events in this process is what is known as supply chain management. Effective management must take into account coordinating all the different pieces of this chain as quickly as possible without losing any of the quality or customer satisfaction, while still keeping costs down.

The first step is obtaining a customer order, followed by production, storage and distribution of products and supplies to the customer site. Customer satisfaction is paramount. Included in this supply chain process are customer orders, order processing, inventory, scheduling, transportation, storage, and customer service. A necessity in coordinating all these activities is the information service network.

In addition, key to the success of a supply chain is the speed in which these activities can be accomplished and the realization that customer needs and customer satisfaction are the very reasons for the network. Reduced inventories, lower operating costs, product availability and customer satisfaction are all benefits which grow out of effective supply chain management.

The decisions associated with supply chain management cover both the long-term and short-term. Strategic decisions deal with corporate policies, and look at overall design and supply chain structure. Operational decisions are those dealing with every day activities and problems of an organization. These decisions must take into account the strategic decisions already in place. Therefore, an organization must structure the supply chain through long-term analysis and at the same time focus on the day-to-day activities.

Furthermore, market demands, customer service, transport considerations, and pricing constraints all must be understood in order to structure the supply chain effectively. These are all factors, which change constantly and sometimes unexpectedly, and an organization must realize this fact and be prepared to structure the supply chain accordingly.

Structuring the supply chain requires an understanding of the demand patterns, service level requirements, distance considerations, cost elements and other related factors. It is easy to see that these factors are highly variable in nature and this variability needs to be considered during the supply chain analysis process. Moreover, the interplay of these complex considerations could have a significant bearing on the outcome of the supply chain analysis process. There are six key elements to a supply chain:

- Production
- Supply
- Inventory
- Location
- Transportation, and
- Information

The following describes each of the elements:

1. Production: Strategic decisions regarding production focus on what customers want and the market demands. This first stage in developing supply chain agility takes into consideration what and how many products to produce, and what, if any, parts or components should be produced at which plants or outsourced to capable suppliers. These strategic decisions regarding

production must also focus on capacity, quality and volume of goods, keeping in mind that customer demand and satisfaction must be met. Operational decisions, on the other hand, focus on scheduling workloads, maintenance of equipment and meeting immediate client/market demands. Quality control and workload balancing are issues which need to be considered when making these decisions.

2. Supply: Next, an organization must determine what their facility or facilities are able to produce, both economically and efficiently, while keeping the quality high. But most companies cannot provide excellent performance with the manufacture of all components. Outsourcing is an excellent alternative to be considered for those products and components that cannot be produced effectively by an organization's facilities. Companies must carefully select suppliers for raw materials. When choosing a supplier, focus should be on developing velocity, quality and flexibility while at the same time reducing costs or maintaining low cost levels. In short, strategic decisions should be made to determine the core capabilities of a facility and outsourcing partnerships should grow from these decisions.

3. Inventory: Further strategic decisions focus on inventory and how much product should be in-house. A delicate balance exists between too much inventory, which can cost anywhere between 20 and 40 percent of their value, and not enough inventory to meet market demands. This is a critical issue in effective supply chain management. Operational inventory decisions revolved around optimal levels of stock at each location to ensure customer satisfaction as the market demands fluctuate. Control policies must be looked at to determine correct levels of supplies at order and reorder points. These levels are critical to the day to day operation of organizations and to keep customer satisfaction levels high.

4. Location: Location decisions depend on market demands and

determination of customer satisfaction. Strategic decisions must focus on the placement of production plants, distribution and stocking facilities, and placing them in prime locations to the market served. Once customer markets are determined, long-term commitment must be made to locate production and stocking facilities as close to the consumer as is practical. In industries where components are lightweight and market driven, facilities should be located close to the end-user. In heavier industries, careful consideration must be made to determine where plants should be located so as to be close to the raw material source. Decisions concerning location should also take into consideration tax and tariff issues, especially in inter-state and worldwide distribution.

5. Transportation: Strategic transportation decisions are closely related to inventory decisions as well as meeting customer demands. Using air transport obviously gets the product out quicker and to the customer expediently, but the costs are high as opposed to shipping by boat or rail. Yet using sea or rail often times means having higher levels of inventory in-house to meet quick demands by the customer. It is wise to keep in mind that since 30% of the cost of a product is encompassed by transportation, using the correct transport mode is a critical strategic decision. Above all, customer service levels must be met, and this often times determines the mode of transport used. Often times this may be an operational decision, but strategically, an organization must have transport modes in place to ensure a smooth distribution of goods.

6. Information: Effective supply chain management requires obtaining information from the point of end-use, and linking information resources throughout the chain for speed of exchange. Overwhelming paper flow and disparate computer systems are unacceptable in today's competitive world. Fostering innovation requires good organization of information. Linking computers through networks

and the internet, and streamlining the information flow, consolidates knowledge and facilitates velocity of products. Account management software, product configurations, enterprise resource planning systems, and global communications are key components of effective supply chain management strategy.

Basics of Supply Chain Management

Role of a supply chain

A supply chain is a network of suppliers and distributors connected via transportation lanes to supply and distribute a product. To be successful, a supply chain must contain a certain number of facilities, the main being production facilities and storage facilities. These facilities are exactly what their names imply—the product is produced at the production facility and then stored at a storage facility. From there, products are shipped via transportation lanes, which are modes of transportation that can be anything from roadways to waterways to airlines.

Impact of a supply chain's efficiency

The success and smooth operation of a supply chain has a direct impact on a company's financial well-being. Failure in the supply chain can include inventory not being produced in an acceptable amount of time, orders that are never placed or shipped, and poorly managed warehouses. For companies that do experience supply chain problems, the average drop in company stock price is 7.5% on the day the problem is announced. Over a 12-month period, six months before the public announcement and six months after, the average stock drop is 18.5%.

Inventory in production facilities

Production facilities typically stock three separate categories of inventory: raw materials inventory, work-in-progress inventory, and finished goods inventory. Raw materials inventory includes materials used to make a product that is not yet complete; for example, paper and ink to produce a manual. Work-in-progress inventory consists of the inventory that is currently in production but not yet finished. Finished goods inventory includes products that are fully assembled and ready to be shipped. Most storage facilities do not hold all three types of inventory. Warehouses typically hold just one type, while distribution centers contain each type of inventory.

FTL and LTL shipments

One mode of transportation used by many companies is roadways, or the trucking industry. An FTL shipment, or a full truckload shipment, consists of a fully loaded truck that is driven to the shipper. An LTL shipment, or less-than-truckload, is typically used for smaller forms of freight. An FTL shipment is often preferred for a number of reasons. It is cheaper to ship a full load of goods than a half-filled truck, and the product is delivered via FTL with no handling in between stops, whereas an LTL shipment typically makes several stops to change trucks. However, FTL can also cause delays in shipping because it requires more finished products.

Operation of a supply chain

A supply chain operation typically consists of demand, supply, and cash. Demand for a product is expressed through orders placed for that product. The demand results in the supply of the product via the various forms of shipment. The products reach their final destination (the demand), where payment (collectively called cash) for the supplies is given to the suppliers for providing them their demands.

Customer and supplier

For an exchange of demand, supply, or cash to take place, there must first be a customer and a supplier. The customer typically refers to the consumers of the product in demand; this can include the customer placing the order or the ultimate consumer, the person who actually purchases it from the store. The supplier, on the other hand, can include the actual supplier of the goods who ships the products to the customer, or it can refer to the person selling it.

Production strategies

The production of goods by a supplier is dependent on the production strategy, of which there are several types, including make-to-stock, make-to-order, and assemble-to-order. A make-to-stock strategy consists of a supplier who makes vast amounts of a product and stores them until orders for that item are placed. Suppliers who utilize a make-to-order strategy make goods as the orders for them come in. Assemble-to-order consists of products that are partially built, but full assembly does not take place until the order comes in. An example of this would be computer companies, who utilize the assemble-to-order strategy so they can customize the computers ordered.

Push chains and pull chains

A push chain typically refers to inventory that is made in advance and then "pushed" down the supply chain to the customers. This references the make-to-stock strategy of production. Pull chains refer to inventory "pulled" down the chain by specific orders. Both forms have their advantages and disadvantages. Push chains can typically deliver goods faster as they are already assembled, but must rely on demand forecasts, which may or may not be accurate, to determine how much they should stock. Push chains, on the other hand, need not worry about too much or too little inventory.

Impact of information on the supply chain

While not referred to as a key component of the supply chain like demand, supply, and cash, information is a vital part of the supply chain flow. Information is present in the supply chain process from the beginning, as orders are information of immediate demand, but is generally exchanged so transactions can actually take place. Information also comes in the form of demand forecasts, production schedules, and announcements of any kind, both good and bad. The flow of information within a supply chain can occur at any time and, unlike other components in the supply flow, is not limited.

Internal and external supply chains

An internal supply chain refers to the facilities that are actually owned and operated by the company itself. An external supply chain refers to the networks outside of the company's ownership. Internal supply chains are preferable because they are generally run more smoothly, as the company has direct control over the process and does not have to buy and sell its own goods. A company owning the majority of its supply chain is referred to as vertical integration.

Documenting shipments

For a business to be successful with its supply chain, it must have clearly defined shipping procedures in place to prevent mistakes that could result in lost business. There must be a purchase order from the customer and a sales order from the supplier (both of these forms contain the same information and terms). In addition to this documentation, each shipment that is sent out must also be accompanied by other documentation, including packing slips, shipping notices, and tracking information. The documents must be traceable for both the customer and the supplier.

Variability

There are many different forms of variability. These include delivery times, production yields, maintenance schedules, daily sales, costs, and demand, to name a few. The more variability, the more difficult it becomes to run the supply chain. To help ensure their products reach the suppliers, businesses cope with variability by alternating suppliers and vendors in the event of a production shortage or delay; alternating transportation sources should the regular ones fall through; quality assurance programs; and forecasting attempts so production can be slowed during times of decreased demand.

Effect of scale

The sheer number of companies involved in a supply chain and responsible for the variability in the system determines the scale of that supply chain, and some supply chains have hundreds of companies all across the world, vastly increasing the system's complexity. Failure to plan for complexity and variability within the supply chain can cause problems within. To lessen the effect of scale on complexity and variability issues, steps should be taken to predict variability through alternating suppliers and transportation sources, quality assurance programs, and forecasting.

JIT manufacturing

JIT manufacturing, or Just-In-Time manufacturing, is a method widely used to reduce expenses while at the same time producing higher-quality products at a lowered expense to the manufacturer. This is done by scheduling the materials to arrive at the warehouses and production facilities right at the moment they are needed in the production process. This is advantageous in a number of ways: It helps to reduce inventory, which in turn reduces holding costs and improves the return on their assets. This requires closely working with suppliers to make sure more frequent or sporadic shipments are delivered on time.

Complexity

JIT manufacturing reduces complexity by reducing inventory in the warehouses and production facilities, as well as by simplifying the ordering and shipping process. Payments are also simplified with JIT manufacturing, as large orders of identical products are placed instead of orders with multiple products. These simpler orders reduce complexity by virtually eliminating the confusion that goes along with ordering multiple products within one order. In addition, these orders are paid for on delivery, reducing the need for more documentation.

Retail replenishment

Supply chains are a key factor in retail replenishment. It is up to the supply chain to have the products to the storeowners on time so they can replenish their stock as it runs low. However, as a result of variability, retail replenishment is often difficult to plan. Traditionally, retailers would manage and stock their own inventory, but consignment is more helpful in this situation because it allows producers to stay in control of their own products, even if they are being sold through a retailer.

Vendor-managed inventory

Vendor-managed inventory (VMI) is a popular option for retail replenishment. As the name implies, VMI is inventory that is managed by the vendor, separating control from ownership. With the VMI process, the retailer gives the producer continuous updates on inventory status and it is then up to the producer to replenish the inventory in a timely fashion. Once the inventory is delivered, the retailer takes over ownership of the products. This is a popular approach for retailers because it saves them money as a result of reduced inventory and eliminates the hassle of tracking that inventory.

CPFR

CPFR, or collaborative planning, forecasting, and replenishment, is a combination of the three programs for which it is named. CPFR relies on the Internet to gather the information needed to coordinate inventory decisions and simplify the movements of goods up and down the supply chain. CPFR directly communicates through real-time data. In addition, trading partners are able to update shared plans and forecasts online, making the entire process easier and faster. Although CPFR is a technologically advanced program, it requires expensive equipment and systems that some companies are reluctant to invest in.

Drawbacks of retail replenishment programs

While many retail replenishment programs such as CPFR, VMI, QR, and others have been touted as major money and time savers, recent studies have shown that they may not be as efficient as some suggest. Some studies have shown that companies applying these programs experienced a very slight reduction in the amount of inventory in their warehouses and holding costs. Other companies experienced no reduction. The industries that fared the best were those who implemented retail replenishment programs with a number of other inventory-reducing strategies.

Zero-sum game

Trading partners often compete with each other over the relative shares of a fixed amount of money. When this happens, two parties within a supply chain compete to see who can win the largest share. This is called a zero-sum game. Sometimes, though, parties cooperate rather than compete. This is the more favorable situation, because in this case both of their combined profits are improved as they work together rather than fight over an already-fixed sum of money.

Virtual integration

Virtual integration is a form of collaboration. Collaboration allows companies to cooperate with each other for the common goal of developing a complete supply chain. This approach is used to integrate members of the supply chain together without sacrificing ownership. When this takes place, partnership agreements between members of the chain are formed. This is a good start, but for it to be true virtual integration, all members of the supply chain must coordinate the chain's three flows across the entire chain.

Business cybernetics

Cybernetics is the study of the components that make up one complicated system. This can apply to all sorts of things, from computers to human beings to animals to supply chains. In the business world, cybernetics breaks down a subject's various principles to understand it better. One factor in business cybernetics is turning inputs into outputs; for example, a bicycle business might take all the parts required to assemble a bicycle (the input) and turn it into something that can be sold—a bike (the output).

Extrinsic and intrinsic factors

Intrinsic factors are those influences within a supply chain that a firm or manufacturer can control, such as the amount of product made or its price. Extrinsic factors, on the other hand, are those influences that are out of the firm or manufacturer's control, such as weather that affects a shipment or a natural disaster that destroys all the goods within the plant. Such extrinsic factors can have a very adverse effect on a supply chain.

Key processes in managing systems

The three main processes in managing systems are understanding, prediction, and control. Understanding is the first step and involves having a working knowledge of the system so you can predict how it will respond to certain changes, such as extrinsic factors. Prediction, which takes the form of such things as forecasting statements, helps you gauge how to react to changing factors. These predictions then lead to the ability to control the system itself. These processes are generally prioritized by first understanding, then prediction, then control, although, in practice, these priorities are often reversed.

Relations

Linear relations
Relations refer to the way input and output values are mapped on a graph. Linear relations map the inputs to outputs in a straight line. This is the most preferable of the relations forms because everything involved with it, from understating to prediction to control, is simple and follows a specific form: Increasing the input will always result in the same increase in the output. This is the only form of relation that is considered linear.

Monotonic relations

Relations refer to the way input and output values are mapped on a graph. One of these relations is monotonic, with which predictions are shaky at best. There is one constant with a monotonic relation, and that is that increasing the input will not reduce the output. The shape of the curve from there can and will vary from a steep climb to a slow drop. A monotonic relation will often take the form of a curve that doesn't increase until a specific limit is reached. From there, it often rises quickly.

Change with continuous relations

With continuous relations, the output will either rise or fall with changes in the input. This occurs continuously (hence the name) without sudden jumps or jerks in the line. Continuous relations also make it difficult to control the output, because the increasing input can have any kind of effect on the output, be it making it higher, lower, or stagnant. When mapped, a continuous relation will often rise steadily, peak, and then steadily fall again. This is often seen in the relationship between price and the resulting profit; as the price continues to rise, the profits fall.

How single-valued relations change

Single-valued relations, one of the more common relations within supply chains, produce an erratic change in which the actual outcome is difficult to predict. With a single-valued relation, the only consistency is that an input will always result in the same type of output. After this, any type of change in the input can result in a dramatic change in the output. In addition, there is rarely a smooth change in between like there is with a continuous relation.

The impact of phase shifts on supply chains

Delays in the systems are a normal occurrence and can happen in demand, supply, and cash, all at once or separately. They range in length of time and can be over quickly or drawn out for weeks. Delays, however, can result in phase shifts, which cause a great deal of confusion in the supply chain as there is almost no way of determining if delays are common delays that occur regularly, or if they are indicative of a bigger problem within the system. This is because the original demand is very irregular in its signal.

Feedback

Positive feedback

Positive feedback occurs when a system's output is increased in turn increasing movement. The incoming strength of the signal continues to increase over time if it is not balanced out, which can result in a system overload. Positive feedback, when kept in check, has a positive effect on a system because it fuels movement and increases growth within the system. Keeping positive feedback in check requires workers to carefully modify the inputs and then analyze the resulting outputs.

Negative feedback.

Negative feedback is the result of decreasing the output of a system in a particular direction with the goal of decreasing the movement and activity within the system. Despite the connotations that go along with its name, negative feedback is necessary to keep a system in balance. Negative feedback keeps positive feedback from overloading a system and in turn keeps it stable by keeping it within a set area of bounds. Negative feedback is most often seen in the design phase of systems.

Importance of feedback

Feedback is essential for the supply chain because it provides the information necessary to learn how to better regulate the system's output. Feedback also works to keep systems in check and prevents them from becoming too overloaded; assists with the flow of goods down the supply chain in a smooth and constant pattern; and gives companies advance information, allowing them to make better, more accurate predictions with regard to supply and demand. This in turn results in increased savings and better information.

Modeling a supply chain

The main benefit of modeling a supply chain is that it simplifies a complex process, and models are useful with all three of the key processes (understanding, prediction, and control). Modeling promotes a thorough analysis and understanding of the system and the main components that keep it working. In addition, models assist in helping predict how the system will react to a number of circumstances and conditions, and they are helpful in controlling real-world systems.

Three categories of models

The majority of models can be categorized into one of three categories: conceptual, mathematical, and simulation. Conceptual models represent the chain through the use of diagrams and descriptions, and then reach conclusions through verbal reasoning. Mathematical models use formulas and procedures to represent the supply chain, and come to their solutions by solving and applying their formulas and procedures. Simulation uses representations of objects and interactions, and then finds solutions through experiments. Each of these models is useful for different situations and outcomes.

Conceptual models

Considered the simplest of all the models, conceptual models represent the chain through the use of diagrams and descriptions, and then reach conclusions through verbal reasoning. This is a formal type of model that is most effective when trying to achieve a realistic assessment. Detailed diagrams help to simplify the supply chain process, then verbal explanations accompanied by real-life examples explain the diagrams and descriptions. The most effective form of conceptual models utilizes a mixture of detailed diagrams and an assortment of verbal explanations to help reach a common understanding.

The strengths and drawbacks of conceptual models

The main strength of a conceptual model is its ability to explain the complex processes that go along with supply chains. However, it has a poor ability to predict and control occurrences in the chain. For this reason, conceptual models are usually used for the explanation portion of the system, while mathematical and simulation models are used to explain the more complex processes that a conceptual model fails to illustrate or explain.

Parameters in the mathematical model

Mathematical models use formulas and procedures to represent the supply chain, and come to their solutions by solving and applying those formulas and procedures. A parameter in the mathematical model involves setting the value of a specific quantity before the analysis is carried out. Determining the values of parameters is a fairly flexible process, as they can either represent inputs or outputs in the model. Parameters are determined based on the information the grapher already has.

Simulation model

A simulation model is most commonly used to determine the most realistic assessments of the supply chain. Simulation models are more realistic than mathematical or conceptual models and, when done correctly, are the most effective at modeling supply chains. Rather than breaking behavior down into formulas, equations, and diagrams, a simulation model instead uses objects to model real-world objects. Commercial simulation tools allow for the most accurate simulations, although simulation models can be much simpler in design.

Monte Carlo method

The Monte Carlo method is a form of experimentation used in simulation models. With the Monte Carlo method, a model is run a number of times with a variety of random values to identify the role that chance plays in the simulation outcomes. This variety results in a more accurate simulation. By studying and then comparing the different outcomes shown from the Monte Carlo method, companies are better able to identify problem areas and then work to make the necessary improvements.

Who should be in charge of modeling systems

For each type of model to be effective, it must be done correctly by someone with the necessary training and experience. For this reason, many managers don't feel qualified to do modeling themselves, even though it is one of the most effective ways of better understanding processes and utilizing management talents and roles. The best modelers are those who are familiar with all three systems, so they are able to analyze which model best fits a company's needs. That said, managers within the company are usually the most proficient with conceptual models, as they know them better than anyone.

Optimization and the benefits of linear programming

Optimization is the ability to tell a person what inputs to use to produce the best, most effective output. Several techniques for optimization exist in supply chain management, the most common of which is linear programming. Linear programming puts all relationships between inputs and outputs in a linear form, making them easy to understand. Linear programming can be done in a number of ways, including in Excel, which even has a built-in optimizer for the express purpose of linear programming. It can also be done with a number of planning tools.

Software

Supply chains are best designed and managed via software that has been designed specifically for that purpose. A number of different types of software are used in supply chains; they vary in price, features, and capabilities, and choosing the right one can be a daunting task. They range from basic manufacturing systems to complex applications that are tailored to solve specific problems within the supply chain. A great deal of research and knowledge of your own supply chain is necessary for picking the right software.

ERP system

Enterprise Resource Planning is the preferred software for the majority of manufacturing companies in the U.S. For the most part, the applications revolve around the internal operations of manufacturing. The ERP system's main strength is its detailed planning modules that help to manage supply, production, and distribution. In addition, they also help with purchasing, receiving, and sales. While ERP is beneficial to many companies, it is lacking in that its main focus is primarily on one production facility, instead of the multiple facilities that make up a supply chain.

 APS system

The Advanced Planning System was designed specifically to manage supply chains. APS systems typically focus on the implementation of planning and design, as opposed to ERP, which focuses on planning and operations. Although modules for each APS system vary, they typically include network design, master planning, production planning, scheduling, materials and purchasing planning, demand planning, and fulfillment planning. When compared to an ERP system, an APS provides such advantages as a more flexible scheduling system and mathematical applications that support the optimization of the supply chain.

Transportation management software

The most advanced and successful transportation software systems include the means for tracking shipments and orders, scheduling drivers, calculating costs for deliveries, and tracking gas mileage, among other things. This sort of software helps to cut costs and track expenditures. However, it's important to remember that transportation software is not one size fits all, as shipping requirements and costs are different for trucks than for air cargo.

Internet-based systems

Many supply chain companies are opting to manage their business through Internet-based systems. This is advantageous for a number of reasons, but mainly because information is transmitted much quicker via the Internet. Demand and cash flow, two supply chain processes, can be moved exclusively through the Internet. Electronic fund transfer and data compressed into PDF files or other forms of electronic files are tracked and transmitted much faster and easier with Internet-based systems. All functions used in supply chains, except for the actual moving of the products, can be done faster through the Internet.

XML

XML, or Extensible Markup Language, makes communication via the Internet easier by supporting complex data structures. It gives each piece of data a tag that labels it correctly, making it possible for the machines to read Web pages. XML is easier to use than XML-formatted languages because XML doesn't require anything more than software, whereas XML-formatted requires computer programmers. XML virtually eliminates the need for humans with some applications by allowing these interactions to communicate with each other over the Internet. XML is becoming more popular and more widely used.

Impact of the Internet

Through the use of XML, which makes human interaction with computers a thing of the past, and Web services, which make it possible for software programs to tap into other programs, the Internet is making supply chain management faster, easier, and more accurate. It allows human beings working on supply chains to focus on more important upper management issues instead of being bothered with medial chores such as placing orders and tracking shipments, which can now be done via the Internet.

Design tools

The three different types of models (conceptual, mathematical, and simulation) all focus on using models and diagrams to effectively explain complex processes. Most of the time, users can find tools for making these diagrams within the APS systems. However, many different types of software focus specifically on the design of models and the way the supply chain looks in print. These applications make realistic, professional diagrams that can greatly aid a supply chain in its operations.

Future of the ERP and APS systems

Enterprise Resource Planning and Advanced Planning and Scheduling both have useful applications and modules, and both are for supply chain management. Some have suggested that implementing the two systems together by linking APS systems to ERP systems would be the best option for successful supply chain management. This is a complicated process, and they are not compatible programs in all areas. However, some companies have already successfully integrated APS with ERP and have had good results with the process.

Order and tracking

An order is usually comprised of a number of different products, so companies generally use a variety of means to keep track of them for filling and shipping purposes, such as UPC codes, product or part numbers, or SKU numbers. As these various identifiers are usually customized to each industry and even company, manufacturing companies must take care to provide detailed specifications of each order to avoid confusion and delay. In addition, companies who conduct business internationally must adapt to various measurements, such as the metric system.

Shipping orders

Typically, an order will be sent to multiple locations. For example, a grocery store may place an order and have it shipped to various locations throughout the country. Transportation services must also take into account a number of other factors when shipping, including receiving hours and docks, to name a few. Companies that have more than one plant generally also need to have a distribution center for products that are to be merged in transit.

Delivery time

In the manufacturing industry, prompt delivery time is important, especially as businesses and organizations work to reduce their own inventory. As a result, a shipment that arrives too early can throw the entire inventory out of order. Delivery times are not specified by dates; rather they are handled in intervals of time, generally blocks of about an hour. Some receiving companies are quite strict about punctuality and will charge suppliers if a delivery is late. Some companies opt to have each item in the order scheduled separately, while others prefer their entire order be shipped at once.

Parts of an order

The typical order is a document that can be divided into three basic parts: a header, a body, and a footer. The header involves the specifics of the order and lists them in line items, such as the customer, payment information, and order and delivery dates. The body contains the items of the order and is organized by quantity and price per unit. The footer of the order contains financial totals, such as order total, sales tax, and delivery charges. More lines or extensions may need to be added if orders are to be delivered separately.

Progression of processing an order

In the past orders were communicated by either phone or postal mail, but now an order can take place via phone, fax, Internet, or EDI (electronic document interchange). These technological advances have significantly sped up the entire order process. While an order placed by mail could take days, the progression leading to fax machines and the

Internet has simplified the process as well as ensuring greater accuracy and faster processing times.

EDI

Electronic Document Interchange, or EDI, is a protocol that has simplified the order process immensely, eliminating the need for lengthy mail processing by placing and processing orders over private networks in just a few seconds rather than a few days. Companies that use EDI technology also eliminate the need for manual entry, as the orders are sent directly to the processing systems. This takes processing an order one step beyond the Internet—while the Internet is able to process an order in seconds as well, most companies who take Internet orders print them out and manually enter them into the system.

Steps in processing an order

First Step
The first step in processing an order typically consists of verifying and validating order information. Software programs are generally able to catch such errors as erroneous numbers or letters where numbers should be. They also review the individual line items of the order to verify everything is correct. If a company is a repeat customer, their information will be verified as well.

Configuration with regard to order processing
The second step of an order, called configuration, is not always required. Configuration is reserved specifically for orders that are used together. Configuration consists of two checks: compatibility, which checks to make sure the products will work together; and completeness, which guarantees the customer receives all the necessary components. A good example of this would be hardware products in ready-to-assemble toys or furniture, which require a number of screws and bolts to properly assemble. Configuration simply guarantees all the necessary parts are there.

Pricing

The first step in pricing an order is determining the unit price, which entails pricing products according to region or market, as they can vary from coast to coast. The second step is to apply any discounts, which can come from company policies or agreements with customers. The third step is to compute the extended price, which can be fairly complicated but involves specific quantity discount schedules and determining if more discounts apply. The fourth and final step is to total the additional charges, such as taxes, shipping fees, and tariffs.

Checking credit

When an order has been processed and pricing computed, companies must verify that the customer has adequate credit to cover the order total. Most companies utilize a credit management system that assigns each customer to a set amount of credit. The purchases are simply subtracted from the credit total, but this process is often entangled with complications that arise from integrating accounting and order management. Most companies approve an order unless the customer has a "credit flag" from a previous order.

ATP and CTP

Companies have various means of making sure an order is in stock before filling the order and accepting payment for it. One of these ways is ATP, or available to promise, which involves checking both current and planned made to stock inventory to ensure that the order can in fact be shipped. Orders that are CTP, or capable to promise, on the other hand, are used mostly for products that are assembled to order. In this case, the company checks the plant to make sure the products are CTP.

APS system

Advanced Planning and Scheduling systems help ensure that orders are either available to promise or capable to promise. The APS system not only checks the company's inventory, but also checks inventory from other sources and determines whether or not the product can be found elsewhere or delivered via an alternate route. Companies that use APS systems have a distinct advantage, as they can improve their ability to win bids from a proven track record of following through on their commitments.

Typical warehouse

Because of the need to house a large number of goods as well as the importance of being able to fill orders quickly and efficiently, many warehouses are set up with five main areas: the receiving dock, the bulk storage area, the picking area, the assembly area (depending on the warehouse there may be multiple assembly areas), and the shipping dock. The arrangement of these areas is usually linear to accommodate a high number of pallets being moved continuously throughout the warehouse, either in receiving or in shipping.

Picking an order

The first step in assembling the products for an order is referred to as "picking" the order. Warehouses have pick lists that include the items and quantities in the order. This list arranges items in such a way that the employee gathering the items can do so in the fastest way possible, important because picking order accounts for a large percentage of labor. Depending on the size of the product and the quantity, picking the order items can be done by hand or by trucks, loaders, or any number of other types of equipment.

Packaging an order

Packaging an order typically consists of three different levels at most, although not all companies will utilize that many. First, there is the primary package. This is the container that holds the product, usually a box, crate, or can of some sort. The secondary package is a carton that groups certain components of the order together for easier handling. The third layer is the transport packaging and consists of protective packaging, such as bubble wrap or special polyurethane sheets designed expressly for shipping.

Problems associated with shipping an order

A company can run into a number of problems when shipping orders to various destinations. The most common of these is determining the best and shortest route. Route planning must take into account the problems associated with metropolitan or high-traffic areas; in some cases, what would appear to be a longer route actually takes a shorter amount of time during rush hour or other high-traffic times. In cases such as these, timing is another important factor.

Orders in transit

Orders that require shipment from more than one facility are referred to as orders in transit. When this is the case, companies generally opt for a merge in transit. Here, the shipments are sent to one single distribution center and delivered all together in one delivery. This is done through cross-docking, which moves the products straight from the receiving dock to the shipping dock without having to store them in between. Merge in transit is the most cost-effective way of shipping orders in transit.

Customer's payment

Billing the customer for the goods first requires determining the amount, which is usually by either weight or unit price, and then creating an invoice that details the payment information. By law, invoices must include the customer's purchase order and the supplier's sales order. When collecting payment, customers often wait as long as possible to pay. As a result, companies typically opt for a payment in terms such as "2% Net 30," which means that payment is required in 30 days, but a 2 percent discount will be given if payment is made within 10 days.

Radical change

Radical change involves doing away with previous means of doing business and coming up with a new, or radical, way of expediting orders or receiving payments. Radical change is said to be easier to implement among customers. Instituting instant payment is one example of radical change. This eliminates the need for a standard agreement, such as "2% Net 20," and automatically debits the customer's account upon receipt of the products. This reduces busy work and speeds up the entire process.

Incremental improvement

Incremental improvement refers to making small changes to a process that is suffering or not producing the desired results. This approach often fails because convincing customers to see the company's/vendor's point of view can be difficult. These incremental improvements, which can include anything from automating orders to eliminating order confirmation, are often costly and, in many cases, it would be more cost-effective to opt for radical change instead.

Distribution center

A distribution center is a location where raw materials, partially finished, or finished products are temporarily stored during some point in the supply chain process. In addition to storage, products are often sorted, assembled, and packaged at distribution centers as well. Distribution centers make large retail chains possible and allow stores to save money by ordering large numbers of products from their suppliers and having the orders shipped to just one place. From there, the product is distributed to the individual stores either by the retailer or through the use of a third-party logistics provider. Distribution centers eliminate the need for suppliers to ship orders to each individual retail outlet. They also eliminate the need for individual retailers to store more than is necessary at each location.

Warehouses and distribution centers

Warehouses and distribution centers are both locations that hold products or materials at some point in the supply chain. However, the purpose of a warehouse is simply to hold inventory that, for one reason or another, is waiting to move on to the next step in the supply chain. For example, a manufacturing center may produce 1,000 units of a certain product. If a retail outlet places an order for 500 units and the other 500 units have yet to be sold, half the units will most likely be shipped to the retailer's distribution center, while the other half will go to a warehouse to be held until sold.

Supplier

When discussing supply chains, the term supplier has two basic definitions. The first, broader definition of a supplier is the role in any transaction between any two links at any point in a supply chain that supplies the product or material being transferred. In this definition the supplier can be thought of as the opposite of the customer. The second, more specific definition of a supplier is any entity that provides the raw materials necessary to begin production. In this definition the supplier is at the very beginning of the supply chain and does not refer to anyone or anything further down the chain.

Supply chain management

The duties of those involved in supply chain management consist of planning, implementing, and controlling all aspects of the supply chain with the purpose of minimizing costs while maintaining customer satisfaction. Usually, supply chain management is conducted with a specific approach or strategy to maintain all operations of the supply chain as efficiently as possible. In the past few decades many firms have turned to supply chain management as their next step in attempting to boost profit margins and be able to stay competitive in the marketplace.

An inefficient supply chain can negatively impact a firm of any size.

Systems approach

A supply chain is comprised of many different parts and processes, all of which are interconnected at some level. In many cases, each step in the supply chain is dependent upon the preceding step. Because of this interdependence, it is often inefficient or impossible to cut costs by making changes to just one step in the chain. Therefore, most supply chain management strategies take a system-wide approach to the supply chain. To improve the supply chain it is looked at as a whole; any changes that are made must take into consideration every single step and process in the supply chain. This systems approach is also the only way make big changes and, consequently, to have a big impact on the supply chain.

Global optimization of supply chains

A supply chain is more often than not a very complex network of people, companies, and facilities with components spread across vast geographic areas and, in many cases, throughout the world. Each piece of the supply chain often has different and/or conflicting objectives. Supply chains are also dynamic, meaning that over time the supply chain evolves to accommodate changing demand, capabilities, new technologies, and the shifting relationships between all the parts of the chain. In addition, cyclical variations and trends over time have an impact on what the best overall strategy for a supply chain is at any given moment.

Conflicting objectives of a supply chain

The conflicting objectives of each component of a supply chain are the result of the unique nature of each specific component or facility and how they relate to one another. For example, manufacturing facilities operate more efficiently if they can produce the same product in the same way over an extended period of time. However, if the consumer's demand for products changes often, then the retail outlet's needs are in conflict with the manufacturing facilities' needs. As a result, the most efficient way to run each component of the supply chain separately is not the most efficient way to manage the supply chain as a whole system.

Uncertainty in the operational environment

Supply and demand is in a constant state of fluctuation, and manufacturers must commit to certain levels of production long before actual demand can be determined, so aligning supply and demand is difficult. In addition, with typical supply chain management the levels of inventory and back-orders vary greatly. This leads to distributors attempting to even out these levels after it is too late, causing the inventory and back-order levels to vary more than actual consumer demand does. Another contributing factor is that forecasts of consumer demand are never 100 percent correct, making it impossible to predict a truly accurate demand for any specific product.

Strategic level

The strategic level of supply chain management refers to the long-term goals of the firm and the strategies and decisions that are implemented to achieve these goals. The decisions made have an effect on the direction of the firm and its supply chain, not only in the present, but over the course of many years. The components of the supply chain covered by the strategic level of planning usually include size, number, and location of warehouses and distribution centers; the building and design of new manufacturing centers; and the overall strategy for managing the supply chain as one system.

Tactical and operational levels

The tactical level of supply chain management covers the medium range goals of the firm. The tactical level strategies are usually reviewed or updated on a quarterly or yearly basis to maintain the best and most up-to-date strategy possible. Decisions made at the tactical level usually include purchasing and production quantities, desired inventory levels, and any other changes to transportation strategies. The operational level of supply chain management deals with the necessary day-to-day operation of the supply chain. Decisions made at the operational level usually include scheduling of labor, truck loading, and dealing with anything that comes up that needs to be resolved immediately.

Network planning

When discussing supply chain management, network planning refers to the decisions that need to be made when major changes take place within the supply chain. Network planning can also be used when organizing a new supply chain. The purpose of network planning is similar to that of supply chain management as a whole in that the goal is to establish a network that can reduce costs by running as efficiently as possible while still maintaining an acceptable level of customer satisfaction. The term network planning can also be applied to other parts of a supply chain, such as the distribution network, transportation network, or supply network.

Inventory control

Inventory control is the method by which a warehouse or retail outlet manager decides how much of each product, or inventory, he or she should have on hand at any given time. Because keeping inventory on hand costs money, any unnecessary inventory that is held is considered a waste of money. The goal of inventory control is to decide exactly how much inventory needs to be held, and then determine ways to reduce the unnecessary amounts of inventory.

There are many reasons warehouses and retail outlets hold inventory, such as uncertainty in demand, reliability, and timeliness of receiving new orders, and the perceived availability of the product in general.

Supply contract

A supply contract is an agreement between two links in a supply chain that sets forth the relationship of the two parties, such as that of a raw material supplier and a manufacturing center. These contracts usually detail pricing, lead times, quality, and other pertinent information. In supply chain management, supply contracts usually incorporate only the two links in the chain involved with that particular stage of the chain rather than taking the supply chain in its entirety into consideration. When attempting to find the best strategy for optimizing a supply chain, the specifics of these contracts must be analyzed closely to determine the terms that benefit the supply chain as a whole while still satisfying the two parts of the chain the contract affects the most.

Distribution strategies

A distribution strategy is the method by which a firm moves its product from manufacturing centers to the actual customers or retail outlets. In the traditional distribution strategy, products are sent from the suppliers or manufacturing centers to a central warehouse. The goods are then stored in the central warehouse as inventory and shipped out to customers or retail outlets as dictated by demand. Newer strategies, however, now help cut costs by eliminating unnecessary inventory and warehouse space as well as save money on shipping by making each truck load as full as possible. The distribution strategy that is best varies with each firm and depends mainly on the size of the organization and the nature of its product.

Supply chain integration

Supply chain integration is one method used to increase the efficiency of a supply chain by getting all the individual parts of the chain to work toward the overall good of the entire supply chain rather than only working toward what's best for each part individually. Each department of a supply chain should be interested in getting involved with supply chain integration. If the entire chain is running in an efficient, organized manner, each part of the supply chain in turn will benefit. For example, if a supply chain is running more efficiently, the end product may be available to the consumer at a lower cost. As a result, this can lead to more demand and more business for each component of the supply chain.

Strategic partnering

Strategic partnering is one method used to increase the efficiency of a supply chain. When two or more pieces of a supply chain work together to make the chain more efficient, it is referred to as strategic partnering. Strategic partnering is a component of supply chain integration. For example, if a raw material supplier and a manufacturing center come together to determine a more efficient shipping method, or if the supplier and manufacturing center were to share information that made it possible to run their respective organizations in a more cost-effective manner, the relationship between the two links in the chain could be considered a strategic partnership.

Bullwhip effect

The bullwhip effect is the phenomenon of inventory and back-order levels varying greatly when compared to relatively steady customer demand over time. Just like a whip whose tip moves greatly compared to the small movement of the handle, demand, orders, inventory, and back-orders vary greatly the further up the chain one travels from the customer. So while customer demand for a product may be fairly steady over the course of a year, the distributor's orders to the manufacturing centers will vary a great deal throughout the year, and the manufacturing center's orders to the raw material suppliers will vary even more.

Demand forecasting on variability

Supply chain managers use demand forecasting to come up with targets for production and inventory to decide how much product to produce and how much inventory to have on hand. However, because forecasts are never completely accurate in terms of numbers and times, most managers use forecast smoothing techniques to get an estimate that is more accurate with the average demand over time. Also, the more data used in obtaining an estimate, the more these estimates are modified to fit more closely with observed average demand over time. Each of these factors creates variability within the supply chain.

Lead-time

The amount of time an order takes to arrive once the order has been placed is referred to as lead-time. For example, if a distributor orders 100 units of a certain product, it will take the manufacturing center one week to produce the product and one week for the product to be shipped to the distributor. This results in a lead-time of two weeks. This time lapse has the ability to influence any number of existing variability within the supply chain. As a result, the further out an order must be placed, the more uncertainty there will be in forecasting the actual demand for the product at the time of delivery. This uncertainty increases the variability in the supply chain.

Batch ordering

Batch ordering occurs when a retailer or distributor orders a large number of a product at one time. As a general rule, it is much cheaper for the retailer or distributor to order product in a batch, as the manufacturer usually offers volume discounts. Batch ordering can be problematic because the volume discount for the batch order affects the way the order is placed, which in turn portrays an inaccurate perception of what the demand for that product actually should be. This causes the distributor or retailer to place irregular orders with the manufacturer, and introduces even more variability and uncertainty within the supply chain.

Price fluctuations

Price fluctuations put the supply chain out of sync with customer demand by enticing buyers (customers, distributors, retailers) to purchase more of a product when the price is relatively low with the hope of avoiding potentially higher prices in the future, thereby saving money. This causes variability and uncertainty in the supply chain and can lead to too much inventory. Other times, if a distributor or retailer is waiting on a perceived future price drop, it could cause a lack of inventory and a build-up of back orders. Both scenarios can eventually lead to the bullwhip effect.

Order inflation

Order inflation is the practice of not filling orders completely during product shortages. Inflated orders have a damaging effect on the supply chain, as they result in inaccurate data pertaining to actual product demand, which in turn adds uncertainty to the supply chain when attempting to forecast future demand. Order inflation typically adheres to the following process: During product shortages, a product's supplier will sometimes fill only a fraction of the actual order made. In an attempt to receive the amount of product needed, retailers and distributors will often place an order larger than they need if they anticipate a product shortage. This way, when the supplier fills a percentage of the order the retailer still ends up with the amount they require.

Minimizing the bullwhip effect

If a supply chain is experiencing the bullwhip effect, a number of things can be done to minimize its impact. First, uncertainty should be reduced by using more accurate, complete, and centralized data. Reducing variability also helps to minimize the bullwhip effect. Avoiding price fluctuations by negotiating a reasonable constant price is one method of reducing variability in a product. Another way to minimize the bullwhip effect is to cut down on lead-time as much as possible; the longer the lead-time for any product, the more uncertainty is added to the supply chain. Forming strategic partnerships can also minimize the bullwhip effect within the supply chain, as they can share critical information and keep all players aligned to the same goals.

Forecasting

There are three basic rules of forecasting. The first rule states that when creating or using a forecast, one must assume that the forecast is or will be wrong. A small chance exists that the forecast will be very accurate, but in almost every instance the forecast will not exactly equal the actual numbers. The second rule states that the accuracy of the forecast decreases with the amount of time involved in gathering and analyzing data. For example, a forecast for product demand a month from now will usually be more accurate than a forecast for product demand a year from now, as factors change over time. The third rule states that general forecasts are more accurate than specific forecasts. In other words, it is easier to forecast the demand for a certain type of product than for a specific model or brand of that product.

Main categories of forecasting methods

There are four main categories of forecasting methods: judgment, market research, time-series, and casual methods. Judgment methods create forecasts based on the opinions of a variety of experts and professionals within the industry. Market research methods create forecasts using data gathered by studying and analyzing consumer behavior, such as shopping methods and dollars spent. Time-series methods use past examples and data from similar products to forecast future demand. Casual methods build forecasts by using mathematical models based on a wide range of data types to attempt to forecast future demand for products or materials. With casual methods, any type of forecasting method is appropriate and there are no set rules.

Sales force composite

A sales force composite is a type of forecasting tool that falls under the judgment method category of forecasts (judgment method forecasting involves using expert opinions to determine the forecast). With sales force composites, the expert opinions come from the sales force. The opinions of the salespeople are considered valuable because they generally have the most experience dealing with customer demand. In a sales force composite, the sales force's opinions are recorded and then organized to be compared and studied to determine the future demand of the particular product. This is typically not an average; rather, the numbers from the sales force are studied and typically combined with other methods and data as well.

The Delphi method

The Delphi method is a form of judgment method for forecasting. With the Delphi method, individual opinions from industry experts are collected and then summarized. Once summarized, the collection of opinions is given to each surveyed expert. From there, the expert can change his or her own opinion based on the opinions of the other experts who were also surveyed. This process continues until each expert is satisfied with his or her individual opinion. From there, a forecast is produced. This method enables forecasters to separate experts and collect their opinions individually, which eliminates the chance of a dominating expert taking over the group and influencing the final opinion.

Market testing and market surveys

Market testing and market surveys are the two main techniques used to generate forecasts in the market research methods category of forecasting. With market testing, a group of people is gathered together to get their responses and opinions of a new product. These people can either be randomly chosen to represent a broad spectrum of the population or specifically chosen in an attempt to get an accurate representation of a particular market. Market surveys, on the other hand, gather data similar to that of market testing, but instead of gathering a group of people together, the data is retrieved through interviews (both personal and telephone) and surveys from the desired group.

Replenishing inventory

Several methods are used to determine an appropriate time for replenishing inventory. One method is to wait until the inventory is completely depleted. This option often results in a longer lead-time, as customers have to wait for the product to be completed, but it also reduces inventory costs. More commonly, inventory is replenished when it begins to run low.

Periodic review and continuous review in inventory replenishment

In terms of inventory replenishment, a periodic review policy refers to one in which the inventory is counted and tracked at certain fixed intervals. Once the inventory reaches or falls below a preset reorder point (ROP), a new order is placed. With a continuous review policy, however, the product's count is monitored constantly. Once the inventory reaches the ROP, an order is automatically placed.

Thought process maps

A thought process map can be defined as a tool to help you see where your project is headed for the long term. This type of organizational tool is often used in brainstorming sessions to help better organize ideas and come to an overall conclusion of where and when you want your project to go. Thought process maps are said to be successful because they help define a clear objective or assumption, providing further directions and solutions for your project. Thought process maps are ongoing tools and can be modified as new questions, issues, or ideas arise within the life of a project. Ultimately, a thought process map will define a project's objective and how it will be reached.

Process map

A process map, or anything that can be defined as transforming inputs and outputs, helps determine what steps are necessary to transform an input to an output. A process map differs from a thought process map in that, rather than mapping out thoughts and objectives as a thought process map does, a process map illustrates what steps have actually taken place. A process map also includes what is known as a hidden factory, which consists of activities that are not mapped out in the process map but that still occur. This typically includes nonvalue-added work or resources that are overlooked when mapping out a process.

Fishbone Diagram

Used primarily to identify causes of any problems that may arise during a process, a Fishbone Diagram is thus named because when completely drawn out, the shape of the diagram resembles a fish, with the problem being the head of the fish and the categories as the bones that classify and organize the potential causes of the problem. A Fishbone Diagram has at least four categories ("bones") of potential causes of the overall problem, usually falling under the broader categories of manufacturing, service, or administrative. A Fishbone Diagram is most helpful when you have data or statistics to back up these potential problems, but in some cases it is necessary to call on other professionals for their opinions.

Cause and effect matrix

A cause and effect matrix is a tool used within Six Sigma utilized primarily to prioritize process steps to achieve an overall outcome. These processes are prioritized by the needs and wants of the customers to better meet their requirements. Using the ranking system in a cause and effect matrix, users have the ability to explore the impact of certain processes on their own customer's requirements. A cause and effect matrix can also be used to compare the actual process steps with the customer's needs and requirements to ensure that the process steps are properly aligned.

Control chart

Control charts help to determine process variation and identify processes as either in control or out of control. Within the control chart are two main types of variation categorized by assignable cause and unassignable cause. With assignable cause, characteristics include meaningful factors of process, although they may not always be present. The cause can also be avoided, but it should be investigated. In addition, assignable cause variations are not normal to the overall process. For example, a special cause could occur when you are painting or drawing and someone bumps your arm, causing an error. This type of variation is not normal to the overall process. With unassignable cause, variations are always present and caused by chance. They are typically unavoidable in a process, but they are considered normal and should be expected.

The three main components of control charts

The three main components of a control chart are a center line, which is typically the mathematical average of all the samples plotted on the chart; upper and lower statistical control limits, which are points that define the specific constraints of common cause variations; and process values, plotted on the chart over time. Each process put into a control chart will vary. A process can be defined as in control if each process value is plotted within the upper and lower control limits of the chart with no real tendency. Processes plotted outside of these control limits, however, or those that show a particular tendency, are referred to as out of control.

The steps for making a control chart

When making a control chart, the steps include: 1) Select the process that is to be charted. Users can chart multiple processes, but will need to make a separate chart for each. 2) Determine the process sampling plan. 3) Collect data from the process. 4) Calculate the control chart-specific statistics. 5) Calculate the control limits using the proper formula. 6) Make your control chart. Control charts can be constructed through a variety of means and software programs. Once the control chart is made, it is possible to look for variation and special causes.

Six Sigma

Six Sigma is a relatively new concept, the term itself coined in the mid 1980s by engineers for Motorola, which holds the registered trademark for Six Sigma. Prior to the development of Six Sigma, defects were measured in thousands. In an effort to improve the bottom line, the engineers developed Six Sigma, which enabled defects to be measured by millions instead. Since its introduction, Six Sigma has been incorporated by hundreds of companies throughout the world in an effort to lower their in factory defect rates. It is important to note that while Six Sigma itself is still fairly young, a number of its concepts and tools, including charts, histograms, and so forth, were developed and used successfully many years prior to the inception of Six Sigma.

Six Sigma Master Black Belt

The highest level one can attain in Six Sigma is the Master Black Belt. The Master Black Belt exhibits a number of qualities that pertain to sound business practices, including technical and organizational proficiency. The Master Black Belt must have a keen understanding of the Six Sigma mathematical process used to analyze data and come up with statistics. One of the major duties of the Master Black Belt is to train those at the Black and Green Belt levels. It is frowned upon for Green or Black Belts to do any kind of training, and if they must, it is recommended that a Master Black

Belt at least be available to observe and guide the lower level. This is especially true with regard to statistical training.

Six Sigma champion

Six Sigma champions are usually executives or members of management who already have a great deal of responsibility within their business or organization. The main responsibilities of the Six Sigma champion involve shepherding Six Sigma Black Belts. Champions select candidates for black belts and then make sure the Black Belts have the tools and resources needed to perform their duties. In addition, Six Sigma champions have a number of other responsibilities, including selecting projects for Black Belts to implement and then supervising them; making sure the Black Belts receive the support they need by removing stumbling blocks and training them; and monitoring the Black Belts to make sure they are in line with and dedicated to their Six Sigma projects.

Law of the Market

In Six Sigma, the Law of the Market states that the customer's needs and wants define what quality is and that those needs should be the highest priority with regard to improvement. This is important in manufacturing because customer satisfaction is considered to be a chain reaction. The customer essentially provides the means to pay for the entire company, from supplies to salaries. Because the customer is supplying the company or organization with the money, the Law of the Market strives to make the customer's needs and wants the top priority. Necessary capacity or enough employees to complete the work, proper information and instructions, and sufficient resources are all required to fulfill the Law of the Market.

Senior executives in Six Sigma

A major factor in the success of Six Sigma implementation is the support and participation of senior executives and other members with leadership positions throughout the organization. Senior executives should take an active role in mapping out cost reduction plans and then communicating them to the employees, with frequent reviews of work, progress reports, and assessment of whether or not expectations are being met. Senior executives can be present during training or teach training classes, and address the employees themselves when necessary. A successful Six Sigma program is one that includes an active, visible role from higher-ups.

Law of Velocity

Also known as Little's Law, the Law of Velocity is an equation for relating Lead Time, Work in Process (WIP), and the Average Completion Rate (ACR) for a particular process. The Law of Velocity's equation is: Lead Time = WIP (units) / ACR (units per time period). According to the Law of Velocity, by reducing WIP while maintaining the same ACR, the Lead Time is reduced as well. According to Little's Law, increasing the ACR while maintaining the same WIP will also reduce Lead Time. The Law of Velocity is a useful tool for determining an average time frame for expected project completion.

Law of complexity and cost

The law of complexity and cost within Six Sigma states that a product or service that is very complex adds more non-value, higher costs, and more Work-In-Progress (WIP) than processes that are slow or of poor quality. In other words, the complexity of something is more expensive to the organization than something that is of lower quality or produced in a lower speed. One common example of a high level of complexity and cost is the automotive industry. The complex nature of automotive products in general makes it a high-cost industry. Organizations can work to reduce the law of complexity and cost by going back to the basic laws of Six Sigma and working to cut costs in other areas.

Deployment plan

In reference to Total Quality Management, a deployment plan can also be a plan of action. Without a well planned and well thought out deployment plan, many organizations are faced with the failure of the programs they are trying to implement. A deployment plan can include all aspects of Total Quality Management, including training executives and managers, working to improve communication on all levels, working to promote a safer work environment, or it could also be as detailed and complicated as restructuring an entire organization. An organization's deployment plan is most successful when it has support from the leadership within the organization.

Project reviews

Project reviews are important for a successful Six Sigma program for a number of reasons. These include ensuring that Six Sigma tools and procedures are being implemented correctly by Black Belts and Green Belts, and providing accountability to Black Belts and Green Belts while motivating them to complete their projects by having someone to whom they can report progress. For progress reviews to be successful and have their desired effect, they must be conducted on a consistent basis. Goals should be discussed and set in each review, and should include constructive comments as well as address any questions the person being reviewed might have. The overall atmosphere of a project review should be motivational and supportive, with help and suggestions where necessary.

Technical support

Technical support falls primarily under the Master Black Belt's duties. The Master Black Belt should provide any type of technical support the Black Belt needs. For Six Sigma to be effective and address technical issues on a timely basis, the Master Black Belt should meet with the Black Belts on a regular basis to discuss any technical issues or concerns that might come up. This can include troubleshooting technical problems within the scope of the project or any problems that might be obstacles to reaching the final objectives. For this reason, it is important that the Master Black Belts are trained sufficiently in all technical matters.

Full-time versus Part-time Black Belts

Companies must determine whether to implement Black Belts on a full or part-time basis to manage improvement projects. Any time an organization is in trouble or facing some kind of threat, Black Belts should be assigned to project improvement on a full-time basis to oversee the following: customer satisfaction to lower the threat of a lost customer; new products—learning, training, and rolling out a new project by a specific deadline; company stock to mitigate any drop in stock by improving projects and processes; and competition by other companies.

Successful training program

Successful training is crucial to the success of a Six Sigma program. Guidelines for a successful training program include thorough training that doesn't overwhelm. This can be achieved through smaller class sizes, interaction between the Black Belt conducting the training and the students that includes questions and answers, proper use of Six Sigma tools, and testing of the students' recent knowledge in the training to make sure they are absorbing what is being taught. A successful training program will be paced in such a way that students are not overwhelmed, and resources such as pop quizzes or reviews before the beginning of each training session will help instructors to know if the material they are teaching is being comprehended.

Beginning of a Six Sigma program

The organization should be well aware of what Six Sigma entails and what the overall goals of the program are. Some of the things that should be communicated at the beginning of a Six Sigma program include a thorough definition of Six Sigma and why your organization feels it will be beneficial, the objectives the organization intends to accomplish through Six Sigma implementation, the deployment plan or plan of action, and what participation will be required by employees. Throughout the program, communication should include training plans, goals, and project reviews.

Successful improvement project selection

Following are some attributes of a successful improvement project selection: Financial benefit to the business; if a project will not make the organization money, or it will end up costing the organization instead of saving or yielding a profit, it will most likely not be a successful project. The project should have Critical to Quality Characteristics (TCQ), meaning that the project has measurable characteristics that align with customer requirements; ideally, a successful project is one that is completed between four to six months. The project is one in which data can be easily obtained; and through various resources and data points, it has been determined that the project will most likely be a success.

The qualities of a successful project tracking system

Project tracking is essential to making sure projects are being completed on schedule and all objectives are being met along the way. For this reason, a project tracking system should be in place. A successful project tracking system is one that will keep track of all projects, including those that are in progress, those that have been completed already, those that are in review for implementation, and those still being considered. The project tracking system should include the overall results of the completed projects, including inputs and outputs, savings, and cost reduction; the status of each project; and the ability to report on projects. This will allow managers to see when projects have hit a roadblock. A successful project tracking system can also be used as a reference to access past projects.

Successful incentive programs

Incentive programs are used to motivate and encourage workers to complete projects on task and with a high level of quality. In addition, these incentive programs are used to help recruit quality candidates for training in Six Sigma, in particular the role of Black Belt and potential Master Black Belts or champions. Successful incentive programs can include creating rewards that recognize both short-term and long-term goals. They can be cash incentives, gift certificates, and so forth. These are used to recognize effort that goes above and beyond the norm. A successful incentive program will also include those who meet their own individual goals and objectives as well as team goals.

Safe work environment

Providing a safe working environment is crucial in Six Sigma and does not only include physical safety, but the safety to suggest improvements in processes or in the way things are being done. The successful Six Sigma program is one that encourages communication and the resources and tools to approach a manager or other superior when something is out of place or not working. Successful Six Sigma programs do not punish those held accountable for mistakes without first communicating expectations; providing employees with the necessary tools, equipment, and processes to complete their jobs and make improvements; and providing an environment of integrity and respect.

Increase customer satisfaction

Creating loyal customers while at the same time improving your bottom line is another goal of Six Sigma. To increase your customer satisfaction, you should select projects that the customer will see/feel the positive impact from shortly. These are also known as Critical to Quality Characteristics (TCQ), projects that have measurable characteristics that align with customer requirements. Some projects that have successful Critical to Quality Characteristics can include increasing delivery speed, improving the accuracy of orders taken, and improving communication response time to customers.

Number of Master Black Belts needed

The number of Master Black Belts an organization will need is dependent on a wide range of factors, including the number of Black Belts. Master Black Belts, in addition to their other duties, should meet with Black Belts on a regular basis to provide review, training, technical support, and guidance. More Master Black Belts are needed if the organization has many Black Belts. The number and size of your projects is also a determining factor. Sometimes, additional Master Black Belts are needed to help lead large or multiple projects. A third factor is the pace in which you hope to complete your projects. Aggressive completion dates will most likely require more Master Black Belts.

The 5 S's

To implement continuous improvement in supply chain management, there are 5 S's that can assist managers in continually improving overall quality: 1) Straighten up. This includes simplifying the work area and eliminating waste and other materials not needed to get the job done. 2) Sequence. Everything should be organized and tidy; there should be clearly identified and designated spots for all work items. All workers should work together to see that things go in their proper areas when done. 3) Spic and span. The workplace should remain clean, improving not only safety, but allowing workers to take pride in their area. 4) Self-discipline. Workers should have the self-discipline to implement and follow the S's on a daily basis. 5) Standardize. Rules and procedures should be in place and followed.

The benefits of implementing the 5 S's

Supply chain managers who work to implement the 5 S's (Straighten Up, Sequence, Spic and Span, Self-Discipline, and Standardize) throughout the workplace can expect benefits such as reduction in operating costs. Keeping things clean and organized and enforcing rules will cut overall costs with regard to waste and the need to replace lost or broken tools. The 5 S's are also beneficial in improving the overall safety of the plant, particularly with the first 3 S's. Implementation of the 5 S's can also be an effective sales tool, as outsiders will see the effectiveness of the program and the organized, clean nature of the facility. Morale also improves with a cleaner, well-organized workplace and facility, leading to a more productive work space.

The seven steps for implementing the 5 S's in the workplace

The seven main steps in implementing the 5 S's within an organization are: 1) Assign a committee or team to oversee promotion and organization of the 5 S's. Responsibilities will include execution of a plan as well as continually monitoring effectiveness. 2) Announce the plan. Gather all workers together and explain the program with a kick-off meeting or party. 3) Have an initial facility-wide cleaning. Cleanliness plays a significant role in implementing the 5 S's; an initial cleaning and organization will be required. 4) Clean the entire facility. Work on cleaning and organizing areas that are not under management of the 5 S's committee. 5) Focus on continuous improvement. This includes working to constantly identify areas that can be improved. 6) Include management. Management (not those already on the 5 S's committee) should be included in all efforts to implement and improve the 5 S's. 7) Constantly work to improve and involve management.

Scheduling

Leadership

For lean scheduling to be effective within a manufacturing organization, the leadership of the facility and company should be heavily involved because of their impact on its implementation. Leadership and management can impact lean scheduling in a positive manner by providing the proper training and tools to schedulers so they know exactly how to form and implement a lean schedule, and by staying involved to promote an overall atmosphere that emphasizes the importance of lean scheduling. Those in leadership positions should pass the importance of lean scheduling down to their workers, so they too can understand the benefits, allowing everyone to work toward a common goal.

Hidden waste affects lean scheduling

A workplace that has a low amount of waste and non-value-added activities also helps to enforce lean scheduling within a facility. Lean scheduling will only be effective when problems that contribute to waste are identified; otherwise, time is wasted as employees spend valuable time correcting problems that are the result of an unorganized, messy, or inefficiently run plant. Hidden waste can be eliminated in a number of ways, including developing a process flow analysis to identify trouble areas or implementing a 5 S's program. Organizations can modify the 5 S's to better reflect the facility they run, but regardless of what your facility's 5 S's stand for, they should all follow the same general idea.

Time series analysis

A time series analysis is one method of forecasting sales demand. The time series analysis is also used to identify patterns in sales; for example, if sales increase or decrease during a certain month. It helps users apply standard formulas to forecast demand by analyzing sales histories, gathering information about frequent patterns, and then using the observations of these patterns to forecast future sales. Generally speaking, this type of analysis is useful because not only does it help to determine sales for the year in question, but can also be an accurate tool for predicting sales in upcoming years.

Components of forecasting demand

Four main components of a sales history must be taken into account to accurately forecast the demand of a product: the level component, the trend component, the seasonal component, and the random component. The level component is a single value representative of the average sales. The trend component is a straight line reflecting the tendency of sales to either increase or decrease. The seasonal component is a curve showing the highs and lows of sales throughout a given year. The random component has no specific pattern and simply represents the variation in demand.

Dynamic forecasting with static forecasting

Dynamic forecasting is a technique that allows forecasters to continuously update their forecasts based on the current sales. This technique increases the accuracy of forecasts significantly when compared to static forecasting. Static forecasting, which is primarily outdated, is done mostly by hand. This method uses just one forecast throughout the forecast horizon. Forecasting, for the most part, is now completely automated, so companies have the advantage of continuously updated dynamic forecasts. This is important because of the continuously changing nature of business—changes in price, supply and demand, and capacity can all occur in a matter of days or weeks.

Advantages of forecasting

A number of advantages are associated with forecasting the demand for a specific product or service. From a business standpoint, forecasting eliminates predictable variability from future demand, which in turn allows companies to plan more accurately. This allows for great savings in terms of production and reduced waste. When companies don't rely on forecasting, they are guessing at best, and must also be prepared to handle any potential demand that arises by keeping production high and having reserve capacity, even when sales may not be high. At the same time, failure to forecast can result in lost money if an order is placed and sales are not high enough to go through the inventory.

Aggregate forecasting

Aggregate forecasting is a process designed to simplify forecasting by grouping together similar products and customers, resulting in more stable forecasts. The alternative, which is to forecast demand for single products, is costly and counterproductive. Aggregation results in aggregate forecasts, which are actually more accurate types of forecasts because they are based on much larger samples of customer purchasing habits than forecasting single products would show. Many consider aggregate forecasts to be a crucial part of long-term planning but not as useful for short-term forecasting.

Pareto Analysis

Pareto Analysis is a technique that helps determine what percentage of products account for the majority of the sales. Many companies use the "80/20 rule," which states that 80 percent of sales come from 20 percent of the products. Pareto Analysis, however, is considered more formal and more accurate, and uses a breakdown of three categories, dividing them into 80 percent, 15 percent, and 5 percent. Pareto Analysis is used as a consideration for aggregating products into groups. It was named for Vilfredo Pareto, who suggested that 80 percent of the land in Italy was owned by 20 percent of the population. This theory carried over into manufacturing and business processes; for example, 20 percent of your products result in 80 percent of your sales.

Grouping aggregation

Aggregated products are grouped or organized a number of ways. One way to do this is by grouping similar products that are made with the same main parts and that utilize similar production operations. For example, a car manufacturing plant might group all two-seater cars together.

Aggregation can also be done by region, which is helpful as it is representative of customers that exhibit the same type of shopping patterns, as well as seasons and other regional preferences. You can also group into various segments, such as types of buying habits and demand volumes.

Concerns with aggregate forecasts

In some cases, manufacturers have expressed concern over the potential for aggregate forecasts to discard information about individual products that may, in fact, be useful. However, when aggregate forecasts are done properly, manufacturers and suppliers have all the information they need. This is done by using percentages and multiplying forecasts to return the item forecast for any information that may have been lost. Some also believe that aggregated forecasts are not helpful for short-term forecasting because the items will have too much variation in the short term.

Subjective techniques

While time series analysis techniques are very useful in terms of forecasting, they do not always address every issue that arises. For example, time series analyses would prove useless for new products that have no form of sales history. In other cases, different techniques may be needed for changing market forces. For that reason, subjective techniques, which utilize cause and effect reasoning for analysis rather than statistical information, can be considered more helpful. With subjective techniques, more factors that could influence sales and demand are taken into consideration than with other time series analysis techniques.

How subjective techniques work

Subjective techniques reach their conclusions through a number of steps. First, the manufacturer must gather information on all types of business influences that could affect sales. These influences can include the state of the economy, time of year, and customer demand. The manufacturer's decisions regarding pricing also play a role. From there, the effects of these techniques are estimated and the information is used to reach a prediction or conclusion. Factors such as the state of the economy make predictions fairly simple, whereas market factors such as competitor actions and changing fashions make predictions harder to reach.

Hardest products to forecast

Regardless of the method that is used to forecast, some products are more difficult to accurately forecast than others. Some of the most difficult products to forecast are those that are up and coming. Making accurate predictions depends on the cycle each product goes through during its lifetime, including whether a customer wants that product, growth while the product becomes more known, then evened out sales, either steady or declining. The difficulty in forecasting new products comes from the inability to accurately pinpoint these crucial time periods. Overestimating results in unsold product and underestimating can create unsatisfied customers.

Tipping point

The tipping point occurs when an idea jumps suddenly from a slow-growing curve to a faster-growing one. The tipping point was originally used to describe contagious diseases, but it is applicable to any scenario in which something "catches," including crime waves, the stock market, and consumer buying patterns, as discussed here. Tipping points can therefore lead to unexpected increases in demand as well as sudden decreases in popularity, despite steady sales. Factors that could influence a tipping point might include a recommendation from an expert or a successful sales force.

Competitive advantage

A competitive advantage indicates an organization's creation of a system that has a distinct advantage over its competition. This can be achieved in a number of ways, with the main idea being to create customer value as effectively as possible, thereby rendering the organization indispensable to its customers so they won't be easily swayed by the competition. Although an organization can go about creating a competitive advantage in a number of ways, most routes fall under three main categories: differentiation, cost leadership, and quick response. These are also known as strategic concepts. Each strategic concept serves its customer base through different means, whether that means setting itself apart with an actual, more novel product; providing savings; or delivering goods and services faster than competitors.

Competitive advantage

Differentiation refers to an organization's ability to provide a certain uniqueness to its products, thereby setting itself apart from the competition. Creating uniqueness provides some of the most unlimited opportunities for an organization to improve its products and services and distinguish itself from others. Effective differentiation reaches beyond simply improving goods or services by encompassing everything the product or service has that can influence its overall value to its customers. This can include convenience factors, training opportunities, delivery or installation, or technical support and maintenance, among many other things. A successful operations manager will seek to identify everything about a product or service that could potentially set it apart from competition and increase its value to customers.

Experience differentiation

One way a company or organization can seek to set itself apart from its competition is through experience differentiation. This method has proven very successful to a number of organizations. Experience differentiation seeks to engage the customer by appealing to their five senses to immerse them in the surroundings. Creating an "experience" leaves a more lasting impression on a person's mind, making the visit, product, or service more enjoyable. One example of this could be a beauty salon that immerses its customers in more than just haircuts; instead, they could provide massages, drinks, and a soothing atmosphere in conjunction with their beauty services. Themed restaurants have also found success employing experience differentiation, complete with décor, entertainment, and food that transport the diners to another time or place.

Three groups of operational functions

Three main groups make up operational functions under the managing director of the plant or organization: 1) Manufacturing; the manufacturing portion of operational functions includes the actual process of producing the products, as well as how and where the product is manufactured. 2) Engineering, sometimes referred to as development, encompasses not only the elements of design, but also applies to organizations that require the use of a lab. Engineering can also include research. 3) Materials; these consist of everything required to manufacture and create the product, including purchase organization, receipt of goods, and storage.

Role of a supplier

In manufacturing, the supplier is characterized as the one who provides the goods and services, but can also refer to the company an organization uses to purchase materials, parts, or whatever is necessary for production. Manufacturing organizations that have developed good relationships with their suppliers by paying on time, respecting order and delivery times, and honoring contracts can expect a more successful relationship with the supplier that includes on-time, in-stock deliveries. Suppliers, in turn, must work to ensure that their products and materials are delivered on time as promised. They should also have a policy on quality and returns to ensure their customers' satisfaction.

Producer in supply chain management

The producer, or the actual manufacturing organization as a whole, has a number of different stages that contribute to the overall production occurring within the plant. These stages include forecasting the demand for the product, which influences the quantity produced; completing the necessary planning required to carry out production on time; carrying out the manufacturing process of the product, including building basic components or special orders; the distribution of the product once it is completed; and then the delivery of the manufactured product to the customer. To successfully implement this program, a logical and organized plan must be made and followed closely.

Customer service

Customer service is how an organization works to handle the various needs of their customers in a way that is satisfactory to the customer. Customer service covers a broad range of duties and can include following up on deliveries, refunding money, answering questions and concerns, and handling special requests. Specifically in manufacturing, customer service can be defined as the delivery of the product to the customer at the promised time. Customer service can also be defined as an attitude in the way an organization speaks to and handles their customers. Companies use the Customer Service Ratio to measure the effectiveness of their customer service.

Customer service department

The customer service department is comprised of personnel whose main duties are to handle the concerns and issues that arise with customers. A manufacturing company's customer service department most likely will deal with delivery confirmations, complaints, order revisions, and so forth. It is also the customer service department's responsibility to keep the customer informed about various issues, including deliveries, whether or not a product is in stock, anticipated completion dates, and so forth. Technical support is also part of the customer service department's duties, although a company may employ specialized personnel to deal with inquiries of a technical nature.

<u>The basic goals and requirements of customer service</u>

The main goal of customer service is to meet and exceed customer expectations. Not only does this result in continued business and the building and strengthening of business relationships, but it also generates successful referrals. To meet customers' expectations, customer service should adhere to the following requirements: 1) Customers should receive their shipments and orders on the dates promised; if there is a problem, the customer service department should communicate with the customer. 2) Personnel should do everything in their power to resolve customer complaints and concerns amicably. 3) Customers' questions about products and services should be answered competently and quickly.

Inventory

Inventory is defined as the company's supply of materials in all stages of development, including parts, work in process, and the completed product. Also included in inventory are the items required for the production and maintenance of the product. The effect of inventory on the supply chain is gauged through the amount of inventory at a given time. An organization should not have a surplus of inventory, as it is costly and should only be enough to meet customer demand. Determining how much inventory an organization should have at one time is done through forecasting.

Product life cycle

The life of a product from inception to completion is covered in six main steps: 1) Pre product development, which involves the research of new product development as well as how to produce a specific product; 2) Product development, or the actual beginning of a certain product; 3) Testing and introduction, which tests the effectiveness of the product to ensure it is accomplishing its purpose and introducing it to the marketplace; 4) Rapid growth, or sales of the product; 5) Steady state, which examines the trends and seasonal growth of a product and its effect on sales; and 6) Phasing out, where a product is either phased out gradually, abruptly, or replaced with a new product.

Manufacturing process methods

The four main methods in a manufacturing process are:
1. Project manufacturing, which is the production of larger-scale items such as buildings, plants, or transportation items like cars and planes. Reliability and quality are major success factors for project manufacturing.
2. Lot, batch, or intermittent manufacturing involves the creation of products made by passing the product through its various stages in batches (or lots).
3. Line/repetitive manufacturing utilizes an assembly line to produce high quantities of products in combination with sub-assemblies.
4. Continuous manufacturing is continuously produced and outputs high volumes. Examples of this would be gasoline or certain chemicals.

Make to order approach

The make to order approach to marketing does not hold a consistent inventory of identical products; rather, the final order is based on the customer's individual preferences. Manufacturing companies fill such orders by modifying current inventory to customer specifications; using forecast methods to keep a certain stock on hand; or waiting to order the necessary parts and materials until the customer's order is received. This method is typically used with project manufacturing where major equipment is produced; as a result, the lead time is much longer than modifying current inventory, as it requires production to start from scratch.

Remanufacturing process

Remanufacturing consists of taking used or worn-out materials and products and restoring them to like-new condition. This often includes keeping the main frame and appearance, and repairing or replacing only the broken or very worn items. Many companies remanufacture products, routinely offering refurbished items such as computers, car engines, and so forth. Some manufacturing organizations are based entirely on the remanufacturing process. The processes used for remanufacturing are similar to those of other plants, requiring scheduling and production activity control.

Balance sheet

A balance sheet is utilized by an organization's finance department and states the company's current financial state. The balance sheet takes into account the company's overall assets as well as what it owes. A balance sheet has three main components: assets, liabilities, and owner's equity. Assets are everything the company owns from the actual plant to the inventory inside it, as well as cash and other equity. Liabilities are things that are owed by the company. The owner's equity is the overall difference between the assets and liabilities, calculated by subtracting the liabilities from the assets.

Product costs

Any company will typically incur a number of costs. These costs can be categorized in one of three ways—labor cost, material cost, and overhead cost. Labor cost, as the name implies, is the cost for the labor to produce the product. This can be hourly or salaried. The material cost is the actual price of the product, or the in-store cost (higher than the actual cost). The actual cost and the in-store cost are also known as direct costs. Overhead cost is the amount of money required to keep the business running. These costs are not associated with the actual product being produced and typically include such things as the building itself, electricity and other utilities, and the general upkeep of the plant.

Overhead costs

It is important to know how a company's overhead is established; it can be done by first estimating all of the costs for the plant or workspace, also called indirect costs. These include things like utilities and management. After indirect costs are established, the total amount for all of the nonproductive costs is divided among each work center. The way this amount is divided is at the discretion of the company. Next, the overhead charge rate is determined. This is the amount of chargeable hours worked by the company times the overhead. Individual companies must establish what type of work is included in this rate.

Profit

Profit, which is the amount a company grosses after overhead and costs are taken into account, has three main categories—gross profit, operating profit, and net profit. The gross profit consists of the net sales minus all of the direct costs, both fixed and variable. The operating profit can be defined as the earnings a company makes after all other expenses have been subtracted from the gross profit. These expenses typically include administrative costs, salaries, and depreciation. Net profit is the money made after deducting a company's total expenses, including interest and taxes from the overall revenue. Many companies also refer to this as the bottom line.

Enterprise Resource Planning

Enterprise Resource Planning (ERP) is the overall process a manufacturing company utilizes to manage and integrate the various systems used to successfully run the business. These systems and processes include purchasing, production, inventory, marketing, and finance, to name a few. A company typically uses software applications to help them with their ERP, particularly large businesses who manage large amounts of inventory and personnel. These ERP systems make it easier to manage the overall business more efficiently, offering improved scheduling, improved customer service, faster deliveries, more accurate financial and cost information, and better inventory management.

Ten strategic operations management decisions

The ten areas in which operations managers can make effective decisions are collectively known as operations decisions and consist of:

1. goods and service design, which is the design of goods;
2. quality, which determines how to meet customer quality expectations;
3. process capacity and design;
4. location selection;
5. layout design;
6. human resources and job design;
7. supply chain management, which controls the flow of goods and services down the supply chain;
8. inventory, which requires consistent monitoring of customer demand;
9. scheduling, which requires feasible and timely schedules to meet demand; and
10. maintenance to ensure reliability. An operations manager seeks to implement these decisions by appropriately staffing the areas and assigning tasks accordingly.

MNC

A multinational corporation (MNC) is a business or corporation that delivers its products and services or produces them in two or more countries. When an MNC is very large, it has a large impact on the economy of the countries in which it operates because of not only their economic influence in the area, but because of their financial resources that are often used for political purposes. Because of the effect they have on the economy, these large MNCs also play a large role in government, as they can threaten to take operations elsewhere or cease to supply their products. This can have a drastic effect on certain economies. The most effective MNCs are those that successfully recreate smaller versions of their main offices or headquarters in the countries in which they have expanded.

Phases of project management

The management of an organization's projects can be broken down into three main phases. This can occur with projects and jobs that take anywhere from a few days to years to complete. These phases include planning, scheduling, and controlling. The planning phase occurs at the beginning of a project and involves primarily goal setting, defining objectives and the project as a whole, and organizing a team to tackle the project. The next phase, scheduling, is responsible for assigning and relating the various people, money, and supplies to the activities required for the project's completion and determining a timeline. The final phase of project management, controlling, is ongoing. It is responsible for monitoring all of the resources, costs, and budgets required for the project and it revises them as necessary to keep the project within budget and completed on time.

Project organization

Some companies opt to develop a project organization to help manage multiple large projects. A project organization is an organization formed specifically to ensure that existing programs run smoothly and are completed on schedule, all while handling incoming newer projects. This is generally a temporary organization formed of specialists within the field or company, mostly because the job is unique or the company or organization isn't familiar enough with it to handle it adequately. A project organization is most successful when the work is defined with a specific goal and deadline, the project is temporary but necessary, and the work requires specialized skills that personnel within the organization do not have the expertise to complete.

Project manager

The project manager's main responsibility involves making sure that an organization's projects and tasks are completed on budget, on time, and correctly. Often, and organization will have a number of project managers for different departments. The project manager's job involves duties that all ensure the necessary tasks required to complete the project are done on time. This includes coordinating activities and deadlines with the other team members, organizing and conducting meetings to monitor progress, and making sure the overall project meets its goals for quality. It is also the project manager's responsibility to see to it that the project does not go over budget. And finally, a project manager is responsible for directing and motivating his team and making sure they have the necessary resources to complete their tasks.

Work Breakdown Structure

The Work Breakdown Structure (WBS) breaks a large project down into smaller, more manageable tasks. Often, these tasks are subdivided into even smaller tasks, depending on the complexity of the project. From there, they are divided into specific activities and their individual costs. This can become quite complicated, particularly with a large project. The WBS usually begins with the largest project at the top, with the tasks decreasing in size. A typical WBS would have 4 levels, with Level 1 being the project, Level 2 being the major tasks in the project, Level 3 the subtasks from these major tasks, and

Level 4 would include the activities to be completed. Level 4 activities are often the most numerous in the WBS.

Gantt chart

A Gantt chart is used by project managers to help assist them with scheduling a project. Project scheduling involves organizing and then assigning a specific time frame to each activity and task within a project. Charts are a common and low-cost way for a project manager to help schedule. A Gantt chart is one such planning chart for scheduling resources and assigning time frames. A Gantt chart will make sure that all activities are planned, the order of their performance is recorded, the estimated amount of time each activity will take is notated, and the overall time the entire project will take is recoded. A Gantt chart uses horizontal bars for each activity in the project's time line. This nonmathematical charting technique is popular because it is simple to understand and create.

Project scheduling

Project scheduling is one of the most important aspects of project management and serves a number of useful purposes. By breaking down the project into time frames, it shows the relationship of each task or activity to other tasks, as well as to the project as a whole. It also helps those working on the project see which tasks and activities are a higher priority compared to others, enabling them to complete the projects in the right order. Project scheduling also has project managers set realistic goals with regard to time estimates, as well as appropriate cost estimates. And finally, project scheduling identifies critical holdups within the project, enabling the company to better use its resources.

PERT and CPM

Program evaluation and review technique (PERT) and critical path method (CPM), two different project management techniques, both follow six main steps. These steps include: 1)

Define the project and develop a work breakdown structure. 2) Prioritize the activities and decide which ones take precedence. 3) Map out the network that connects each activity. 4) Assign time and cost estimates to each of the activities. 5) Determine the critical path, or the longest time path through the network. 6) Use the network that has been mapped to help with all aspects of the project, including planning, scheduling, and controlling the overall project.

Critical path analysis

The critical path analysis determines the longest time path through a project's network. It is a mathematical equation that is found by calculating two distinct starting and ending times for each activity within the project. These times are: Earliest Start (ES), or the earliest time an activity can begin, assuming everything else is in place; Earliest Finish (EF), the earliest time the activity can be completed; Latest Start (LS), the latest possible time an activity can begin without disrupting other aspects of the project's schedule; and Latest Finish (LF), the latest time an activity has to finish without delaying the entire project's anticipated completion. The ES and EF are determined through the forward pass, which identifies the earliest times, and the LS and LF are determined during the backward pass, which finds the latest times.

Multidomestic strategy

A multidomestic strategy is one that uses an already existing domestic model globally. Franchises, joint ventures, and subsidiaries are all examples of multidomestic strategies. These organizations have a great deal of independence from their corporate headquarters. Multidomestic strategies cater their products and services to the particular country or location, so operating decisions are given primarily to the individual owners. For example, McDonald's alters its menu depending on which country it is located in. In Japan they serve rice; in Germany, beer; and in India, hamburgers that have no beef in them. A multidomestic strategy allows for a better competitive response for local markets.

Forecasting

Forecasting is the process of estimating or predicting the most likely outcome in an unknown situation. With forecasting, the overall goal is to be as accurate as possible in the predictions. Forecasting is used in nearly every profession, and businesses use forecasting techniques to determine a number of things, including placing orders (particularly seasonal orders), stocking inventory, anticipating sales, and timing product releases. There are many different methods of forecasting, some more reliable than others, including time series forecasting, consensus forecasting, and seasonal forecasting. Demand planning, also called supply chain forecasting, utilizes statistical forecasting methods that are more mathematical, as well as consensual methods.

The common types of forecasting

There type of forecasting an organization chooses depends on what they want to predict, be it sales or inventory. The more common types of forecasting include: consensus methods, which seek to get recommendations or opinions from experts in the field—one popular and well-known form of consensus method is the Delphi technique; simulation methods, which use analogs in the form of mechanics or mathematics to reach a conclusion; decision trees, which are graphical representations of the relationships between particular choices; and time series forecasting, which uses historical values or past trend data to predict an outcome. Many businesses utilize a combination of forecasting techniques.

Qualitative methods

A qualitative method of forecasting is one in which a prediction or recommendation is made based on the educated and experienced opinions of experts in the field or those qualified to give their opinion, such as consumers. Examples of qualitative methods include the Delphi method, which uses a panel of experts to give their educated responses anonymously to a series of questions regarding a product or time frame; market research such as surveys, questionnaires, and test markets; and product life cycle analogies, which create forecasts based on the typical life cycle of a certain product. Another qualitative method could be the opinion of someone such as a salesperson or manager based on his or her own experiences.

Examples of quantitative methods

Quantitative methods of forecasting are those that use actual historical data to determine an outcome or average. Unlike qualitative methods, a quantitative method relies on numbers and figures instead of opinions or recommendations; opinions or recommendations are formed only after seeing the data. Quantitative forecasting is also commonly referred to as time series forecasting. Methods of this include moving averages, which determines a forecast based on an average of data points; exponential smoothing, which is a form of moving average as described above, only it includes trends; and mathematical models such as trend lines and log linear models, which can be either linear or nonlinear and are adjusted to fit a time series model.

Moving averages

A moving average is one way to analyze the data in a time series or quantitative forecast. The four main types of moving averages include a simple moving average, a central moving average, a weighted moving average, and an exponential moving average. The main purpose of a moving average is to smooth out the short-term fluctuations that occur in data, which in turn provides a more accurate depiction of long-term trends or cycles. This sort of forecasting method is typically used in the stock market, and can be used in a number of other industries as well. Time frames for moving averages can range anywhere from five days to yearlong moving averages, which are better suited to tracking longer cycles.

Time horizon

The time horizon is the amount of time that a forecast covers. As a general rule, time horizons have three main categories, which are short-range forecasts, medium-range forecasts, and long-range forecasts. Short-range forecasts last up to 12 months, but are usually shorter and are used for things like job scheduling, assignments, and planning purchasing. Medium-range forecasts typically run between three months and three years and are used for sales planning, budgeting cash, and production, as well as analysis of operating plans within the organization. Long-range forecasts are those that last longer than three years. A long-range forecast is used for more lengthy expenditures, such as planning and implementing new products and services and expanding into a new location or facility.

Focus forecasting

Focus forecasting is a forecasting technique that tests a number of different forecast models and then determines the best one for finding out the needed information. A typical focus forecasting involves the collection of data, such as historical sales figures, buying trends, or any number of quantitative data, and then utilizes a number of other forecasting techniques such as a decision tree, weighted average, mean, exponential smoothing, and others to make the desired prediction. Because it takes into account a number of forecasting tools, it is considered one of the more accurate methods of forecasting with a substantially lower amount of errors, provided the distortions are taken out of the data beforehand.

Time-series forecasting

Time-series forecasting is a method of forecasting that uses historical values or past data to determine a particular outcome. Times-series refer to historic values and can be used in virtually any industry. Utilizing a time-series method of forecasting can include researching monthly sales practices to determine how many people to hire in a given month or week, or data that explains the consumption of a particular product so that the correct amounts can be ordered. Time-series forecasting seeks to understand a particular trend in terms of increase or decrease in the long or short term as well as seasonal factors and trends that could have an impact on demand or inventory.

Short, medium- and long-range forecasts

Medium- and long-range forecasts can be identified over short-range forecasts by three main features: Longer forecasts typically deal with more complicated and wide-ranging issues and decisions, such as the opening of a new plant or expanding into a foreign market; they utilize different methodologies than short-range forecasts, which typically apply more mathematical methods such as smoothing and moving averages. Medium- and long-range forecasts rely more on qualitative methods; and they are less accurate, overall, than short-range forecasts.

Trend projections

A trend projection is a form of time-series forecasting. With a trend projection, a trend line fits into a series of historical data points then draws a line into the future. This is used more with medium- and long-range forecasts. A number of mathematical equations can be used in a trend projection, such as exponential, quadratic, and linear, with linear being the most commonly used. A linear trend line is developed via the least squares line, which is determined through its y intercept and the slope, or angle, of the line. This can be done with the equation $y = a + bx$, with y being the independent variable, or computed value of the predicted variable, a being the y axis intercept, b the rate of change in y, and x the independent variable, or amount of time.

Quality

How quality improves profitability

Improved profitability within an organization is often the result of quality. Quality centered processes often result in better products and services as well as more efficient processes. Profitability is then increased in a number of ways: 1) As processes are improved and become more efficient, costs to manufacture or create products go down, thus increasing profitability. 2) Quality results in improved products and services; as such, customer satisfaction results. Customers are not only inclined to continue to purchase the product, but they are also more likely to purchase new products that come out, as well as refer the products to others. 3) Productivity increases as processes are simplified and improved, enabling employees to produce more in a shorter amount of time.

Quality in relation to supply chain management

Quality can be defined in a number of ways but, overall, quality is how an organization goes about finding and taking advantage of ways to continually improve their services, products, and processes. Quality systems and processes work to reduce waste, which saves the company time and money; provide customer satisfaction through well-designed and well-made products, which serves to increase loyalty and often results in referrals; satisfy employees, which results in increased morale within an organization and higher productivity levels; and increase profitability. All factors that play into a quality system should result in an improved bottom line, increased sales, more efficient production, and a higher market share.

Some of the elements of a quality system

Quality systems have a number of elements in common, including: 1) Management. Quality systems share active and involved managers who are committed to improving quality. 2) Support from other departments. Marketing, purchasing, customer service, and production should all be dedicated to improving quality. 3) Customer centered. Quality organizations are centered on knowing and then meeting the needs of the customers. 4) Use of technology. Technological advancements can greatly improve the quality of a system, and a quality system utilizes technological advancements in their favor. 5) Production. Quality systems provide employees with the tools and resources needed to produce quality products as efficiently as possible. 6) Education/training. Ongoing quality is often the result of continuous training and education to improve employees' abilities to produce quality products and services.

Some of the benefits of quality

The benefits of quality extend not only to the financial aspects of a company or organization, but to all those involved as well. Customers benefit from quality because they see possible reductions in price as a result. Employees benefit from quality through greater pride and satisfaction in their efforts on the job. They also benefit through improved processes with improved communication and a lower amount of problems as a result of quality issues. In addition, they have the added benefit of increased the job security from a more profitable company. Overall, the organization benefits from lowered production costs as a result of improved processes and reduced waste and increased profits, which result in a greater market share.

The ISO 9000 series

The ISO 9000 series is a set of standards designed to document and gauge a company or organization's ability to provide quality management and quality assurance. These international standards were implemented by the International Organization for Standardization in 1987 and have been revised as necessary. The series focuses on eight quality management principles, including: customer focus, leadership, involvement of people, process approach, system approach to management, continual improvement, factual approach to decision-making, and mutually beneficial supplier relations. Together, these standards help management determine the overall quality of their quality systems and processes. While it is not a complete guarantor of quality, the ISO 9000 standards are thought of as an effective starting point.

TQM

TQM stands for Total Quality Management. It is a management strategy used in a number of industries, including manufacturing, education, service, and more. TQM seeks to promote quality awareness and assurance at all levels. It actually originated in the '50s and has experienced a surge in popularity since the '80s. Total Quality refers to the attitude and methods of a company as they continually work to meet their customers' needs. The management of this quality, through a variety of means, works to eliminate waste so the processes can be done correctly the first time around. As a result, problems, defects, and wasted time are eliminated, saving time, money, and labor.

The eight elements of TQM

To implement Total Quality Management into an organization, managers are often taught eight TQM basics, which involve key elements for quality: 1) ethics, 2) integrity, 3) trust, 4) training, 5) teamwork, 6) leadership, 7) recognition, and 8) communication. These eight elements are considered vital to successful quality management. The eight elements are often further divided into four groups, organized by their overall function: Foundation includes the first three elements, ethics, integrity, and trust. Building Bricks includes training, teamwork, and leadership; Binding Mortar involves communication; and Roof includes recognition. This organizational structure and further division into groups is commonly taught in Total Quality Management training courses.

Employee empowerment

Employees who are empowered tend to be more efficient and productive in the workplace. Techniques for building employee empowerment include: 1) Encouragement. Encouraging employees through helpful suggestions can empower employees by helping them understand exactly what is expected of them, which allows them to do their jobs with more confidence. 2) Positive reinforcement. Providing positive feedback and praise is another way to empower employees, as people tend to work better when they feel their efforts are being appreciated. 3) Rewards. Tangible thanks or rewards for meeting production goals are a good technique to empower employees and add increased motivation in the workforce. 4) Offer leadership opportunities. Offering employees leadership opportunities, such as supervising a group or heading a project, offers an increased sense of responsibility, leading to empowerment.

The Just in Time (JIT) philosophy

The JIT philosophy is a system companies adopt as a way to increase their return on investment. The JIT method works to reduce costs associated with inventory. When implemented correctly, JIT increases organizational efficiency, improves methods, saves money, and increases the organization's bottom line. A main goal of JIT, as the name implies, is to provide supplies and products to customers "just in time" by holding the inventory for as short a time as possible while being able to supply it to the customer exactly when they need it. Companies that have found success with this system include fast food chains, which don't begin to cook food until the order has been placed, and software companies utilize JIT to decrease holding times.

<u>Some of the benefits of the JIT philosophy</u>
The benefits of a properly implemented JIT method include a reduction in set-up times, which allows employees to focus their time

on other areas that may need more attention; more consistent employee working hours, as the demand (or lack thereof) of a product can help employers to better utilize workers; better supplier relationships, which results in the ability to rely on products and goods to be in stock and in a company's inventory when needed; more efficient flow of goods from warehouses to the public, the result of employees focused on particular areas rather than doing multiple tasks at once, which can lead to decreased quality; and better utilization of employees, particularly those who have been cross-trained and can help improve productivity within the organization.

The Taguchi methods

The Taguchi methods, developed by Dr. Genichi Taguchi, are designed to improve the overall quality of manufactured goods. Taguchi methods are typically applied to the manufacturing field, although other industries, such as marketing and technology, have begun to implement its concepts. According to the Taguchi methods, the customer is the most important part of the manufacturing process, and loss is defined as customer dissatisfaction, which in turn leads to a decrease in the overall reputation of the company. The Taguchi methods center around the customer and believe customer service increases market share. Generally speaking, the Taguchi Methods take a number of elements with different alternatives and determine which combination of elements allows users to determine the positive or negative effects of each element.

<u>The four fundamental Taguchi concepts</u>

The four fundamental Taguchi concepts are: 1) Quality should be designed into the product from inception, not through later inspection and screening. The overall quality improvements should begin while the product is being designed and continue through completion rather than waiting until the end. 2) Quality is best achieved by minimizing deviation rather than failing to conform to specifications. The product should be immune to certain uncontrollable circumstances, such as weather or noise. 3) Quality should not be based on the product's feature, performance, or characteristics. They can be related to them, but should not be the basis of quality. 4) The cost of quality should be measured as a function of product performance variation. The losses, or deviations, should be measured throughout the entire system.

Pareto chart

A Pareto chart is derived from the Pareto principle, which states that for a number of occurrences in manufacturing, 80 percent of effects come from 20 percent of causes. For example, in manufacturing and business in general, 80 percent of sales come from 20 percent of the customers. For this reason, the Pareto principle is also referred to as the 80/20 rule. It also states that 80 percent of problems come from 20 percent of causes. These causes can include machinery, labor, and materials. The Pareto principal is the basis for the Pareto chart, which is often used in manufacturing and Six Sigma to compare before and after situations. After the chart is studied, experts determine the best place to begin working to correct the situation. Pareto charts are also used to determine the costs of storing and replenishing stock.

Flow charts

A flow chart is one of the most basic tools for quality control and helps to find errors in processes as well as allow employers and employees to visualize the processes. A flow chart consists mainly of pictures and symbols in combination with lines and arrows to show the direction of flow. A successful flow chart will not only identify problems, but it will also help those studying it to come to an understanding of a particular process and the origin of its flaws. A downside of flow charts is a lack of standardized symbols, which can make for complicated explanations within organizations or different audiences. Flow charts can be made manually or with the many software programs available.

Histogram

Histograms are the graphic summary of the variation within a particular set of data. The histogram is a useful tool for visually illustrating patterns that may not be discerned otherwise. A histogram graph consists of categories of continuous variables. The value of each of these variables is plotted in bars. Histograms are often confused with bar graphs, but several important distinctions separate the histogram from the bar graph. With a bar graph, the actual area of the bar determines the value of the data, whereas, with the histogram, it is the height of the bar that determines the value of the data. A histogram is useful because it shows the skewed distribution of a particular measurement that manages to stay within its specific limits; without the histogram, it would be difficult to even recognize the patterns.

Check sheet

A check sheet is a form used for collecting and recording data as it is observed. Because check sheets are used at the location in which the data is produced, they are designed to be very simple with quick and easy recording abilities. A check sheet is thus named because data is often recorded using check marks on the various regions within the form. There are five main types of check sheets, including classification, in which a specific quality is classified; location, or the actual location of the quality; frequency, the presence or absence of a particular quality as well as the number of times it appears; measurement scale, in which the sheet is divided into intervals; and a check list, which consists of a basic checklist of items or tasks to be completed that can be checked when they are finished.

Statistical process control

Statistical process control (SPC) monitors a process and its performance through a variety of charts. The purpose of SPC is to identify risk factors and faults as they occur. SPC's main component is early detection. As a result, faults are corrected and eliminated before the end product, which eliminates waste and saves employee time and productivity. SPC greatly reduces the chance of having to refine or rework a product, as errors are caught early on. SPC selects, plots, and analyzes data during all aspects of a process from beginning to end and is considered more efficient than other quality control means because it identifies problems during the process instead of at the end.

Layout for manufacturing

The six main layout designs for production and manufacturing settings are: fixed position layout, which is designed to handle the requirements of projects that are large and bulky, such as machinery or buildings; process-oriented layouts, which handle production for low-volume, high-variety products; office layout, which places personnel, equipment, and offices to offer the most efficient movement of information; retail layout, which is catered to customer behavior in terms of placement of shelves and displays; warehouse layout, which addresses the tradeoffs between the handling of allocated space and materials; and product-oriented layout, which utilizes personnel and machines for continuous production.

What layout design must achieve

For layout to be efficient, whether in retail, production, or office space, it must achieve a number of objectives, including better utilization of space, machinery, equipment, and personnel; allow for an improved flow of information, products, or employees; provide safe working conditions while improving the morale of the workers; promote improved interaction between customers and clients; and be flexible, as requirements may change with the needs of the company or organization. Successful layout designs also allow for the utilization of smaller equipment. For example, retail displays should be movable and office partitions modular. Flexibility in layout design can also be achieved through cross-training workers, maintaining equipment, and using small, movable equipment.

Process control

Process control utilizes information technology to control physical processes, such as temperatures or chemical levels. Typical process control systems work in the following way: Sensors, which are analog devices designed to collect certain types of data, collect the data. They usually read data on a periodic basis, such as once a minute or once a second. The measurements taken are translated into digital signals and sent to a digital computer. The computer programs read the file and analyze the data. Once the data has been analyzed, it is output. This can be done in a number of ways, such as messages or printouts on the computer screen, warning lights, or signals to motors or operators to change certain settings.

<u>Some of the types of process control</u>
Process control comes in a variety of methods depending on the industry and purpose. Vision systems, used in inspection roles, use video cameras and computers to inspect processes, typically those found in manufacturing or food processing. Robots are flexible machines that can hold, move, and grab items and are a good substitute for human workers, especially when the work compromises the safety of the workers. Automated Storage and Retrieval Systems (ASRS) are warehouses that automatically place parts within the warehouse. Automated Guided Vehicles (AGV) are electronic devices, such as conveyor belts and carts, that move parts and equipment. Flexible Manufacturing Systems (FMS) are those that use a central computer to provide instruction to multiple locations.

<u>How process focus works within a facility</u>
A process focused facility is one in which the facility itself is organized around specific processes or activities

that assist in low-volume, high-variety production. This type of process strategy accounts for roughly 75 percent of all global production. Also called intermittent processes, process focused facilities use processes that are designed to provide a wide range of activities and are adaptable to frequent changes. The facilities themselves have high variable costs coupled with a low utilization of facilities, sometimes as low as 5 percent. Facilities with higher numbers are often those that have more innovative equipment, such as computers and systems controlled by software.

Repetitive focus

Repetitive focus is a strictly product-oriented production process. Using modules, which are parts or components that have already been fabricated or made ready, the repetitive process line is, in essence, a classic assembly line. Products prepared with repetitive focus are prepared on a continuous basis. The end product of a repetitive focus can take on a variety of shapes or sizes, depending on the various modules used throughout the line. Fast food restaurants are one example of a repetitive focus; for example, in making a taco, the taco shell is sent down a line where it is filled with modules such as meat, tomatoes, lettuce, and cheese. The end product often varies depending on what the customer has ordered. Automobile manufacturers often use repetitive focus as well.

Economic order quantity model

The economic order quantity (EOQ) model is one of the more common inventory control techniques. Several other techniques must be in place for the economic order quantity model to be in place. For example, the demand must be known, constant, and independent; the lead time is known and constant; the inventory that arrives from the order does so one batch at a time; no quantity discounts will be used; the only variable costs allowed are those of setting up or placing an order; and shortages can be avoided if orders are placed at the correct time. According to this commonly used inventory technique, demand, which is constant over time, increases and decreases at uniform rates over time. When graphed, inventory usage over time, then, has a saw-toothed shape as inventory increases with each order arriving correctly, then drops when the inventory reaches 0.

Basic demand options

The basic demand options include: 1) Influencing demand. Here, when demand is low, a company or organization can try and increase the demand. This is done through a variety of means, including cutting prices, offering promotions, and more aggressive advertising campaigns. 2) Back ordering during high-demand prices. Back orders are orders for goods or services that are in high-demand and, as a result, sell out quickly, making the company unable to sell it at the moment. Instead, they use back orders for those customers who are willing to wait until the product becomes available again. Many companies do this, but it often results in lost sales, particularly if a customer can find the product faster somewhere else. 3) Counter seasonal product and service mixing. With this option, companies will produce a mix of counter seasonal items to be sold at the same time, such as snow blowers and air conditioners.

Basic capacity options

The main capacity options that a company can use for basic production include: 1) Changing inventory levels, in which managers increase or decrease inventory based on the demand for the product or lack thereof. 2) Varying the workforce, which involves either hiring new employees to meet demand or firing employees if sales or production slow. 3) Varying production rates through overtime or downtime. This can meet a high production demand by providing overtime hours for workers, or satisfy a slow demand by cutting hours. 4) Subcontracting. This allows a company to reach capacity through hiring or subcontracting part of the work. 5) Utilizing part-time employment. In this scenario, part-time workers can fill the needs of the company temporarily. Typically, this type of arrangement does not require special training of the part-time workers.

Graphical and charting techniques

Graphical and charting techniques primarily allow planners to compare their projected demand with their already existing capacity. These are commonly utilized because they are simple to comprehend and use. Graphical and charting techniques use several variables at a time. These methods are trial and error, and while they don't guarantee a production plan, they are easy to compute and don't require special skills. The five steps in the graphical method are as follows: 1) Determine the demand for the product or service in each period. 2) Determine the capacity for regular time, overtime, and subcontracting, where applicable. 3) Calculate labor costs, hiring or layoff costs, and inventory holding costs. 4) Take into account any company policies that may affect workers or stock holdings. 5) Develop alternative plans and observe their total cost.

Variability

Variability occurs when there is any divergence from the ideal process that will deliver an error-free product, on time, continuously. Variability can be caused by both internal and external problems, including employees and equipment that don't follow specific standards, are not properly trained, or don't work; inaccurate engineering drawings and specifications; or unknown customer demands. Companies and firms should continuously strive to reduce variability; the less variability within a process, the less waste in the overall system. Companies can take a number of approaches to reduce variability, including increased inspections or the application of the Just in Time (JIT) philosophy, which supports lean production through a series of forced problem solving.

Total Production Maintenance

Total Production Maintenance (TPM) strives to apply total quality management concepts to preventative maintenance. TPM is one of the key factors used in reducing variability and increasing overall reliability. TPM works to reduce variability through a number of means, including employee involvement and accurate and consistent maintenance records. TPM also comprises the process of designing reliable, easily operated and maintained machinery, including service and maintenance in the total cost of ownership when purchasing machines; working to develop preventative maintenance plans that use the best operators and maintenance departments; and training workers to operate and maintain their own machines, cutting down on outside repair and maintenance costs.

Master production schedule

A master production schedule (MPS), also referred to at a master production plan, specifies what exactly is to be made, such as a number of finished products, and when they are to be completed. A master production schedule must be in accordance with the production plan, which defines outputs such as labor hours and dollar volumes in broad terms, as well as inputs like customer demand and inventory fluctuations. The master production plan is useful because it is able to determine the feasibility of the schedule and can tell what is needed to satisfy and meet the demands of the production plan itself. For the MPS to be successful, a manager must follow the master production schedule for a certain period of time, typically the amount of time it takes to complete or produce a product.

Practice Test

Practice questions

1. The advantages of putting a customer in possession of consignment stock are counterbalanced by the negative impact of:
    a. Having to pay for consignment stock at the end of each period
    b. Carrying costs
    c. Streamlined delivery
    d. Having to keep a customer in continuous supply

2. Which of the following four elements of materials supply is NOT attributed to inventory cost?
    a. Stockout
    b. Ordering cost
    c. Carrying cost
    d. Production rate

3. The production component most closely related to and impacted by the amount of WIP is:
    a. Product lead time
    b. Work in progress
    c. Carrying costs
    d. Transportation costs

4. An accounting department should determine the value of WIP as:
    a. The amount paid to the company providing the inventory materials
    b. All carrying, production, and setup costs accrued before the product's or material's use in the next phase of production
    c. The amount accrued in carrying costs only
    d. Ordering and setup costs

5. An inventory costing system may show a sudden, sharp increase because:
    a. Labor costs suddenly increase
    b. Deregulation incurs higher utility costs
    c. Stockouts have a major impact on profitability
    d. A business must find another supplier

6. Inventory costs are likely to be higher in the initial phases of a manufacturing process because
    a. Product lead times are shorter initially, so more inventory is required
    b. Inspection costs accrue as materials or unfinished products are delivered
    c. "Chasing" costs add to inventory cost
    d. Setup costs are highest at the beginning of a manufacturing run

7. With respect to CPIM, which of the following defines and gives the chief aim of APICS?
   a. The Association for Production, Investment, and Control Society purports to provide certifications with the aim of increasing corporate profits by reducing inventory and supply chain costs
   b. APICS provides CPIM certification and refers to the Association of Operations Management
   c. APICS means American Production and Inventory Control Society and provides consulting services to the U.S. Labor Department
   d. APICS is the acronym for the Association of Production, Inventory, and Control Suppliers, with the aim of licensing suppliers who meet certification requirements

8. From the following answer choices, pick the definition that best describes the category of "fluctuation inventory."
   a. Fluctuation inventory is the portion of finished goods inventory that is apportioned to customer demand
   b. Fluctuation inventory is the same as pipeline inventory
   c. Fluctuation inventory is the same as safety stock, or that part of finished goods used to fill spikes in demand for the finished product
   d. Fluctuation inventory refers to the ratio of difference between high and low production outputs of finished product

9. From the following answer choices, pick the definition that best describes the category of "finished goods inventory."
   a. Finished goods inventory is the portion of fluctuation inventory that meets the anticipated customer demand for products
   b. Finished goods inventory is the portion of fluctuation inventory that remains unused in order to fill unexpected demand for products
   c. Finished goods inventory is safety stock used to increase market share
   d. Finished goods inventory is the store of finished goods and is a combination inventory of fluctuation inventory and anticipation inventory

10. The description that best describes the relationship between materials requirements and production planning (MRP and MPS) and raw materials inventory supply is:
    a. Overstatement in production capacity can lead to pipeline bottlenecks.
    b. Overly ambitious production scheduling can lead to raw materials and inventory bottlenecks.
    c. Accurate MRP and production scheduling aid supplier efficiency.
    d. All of the above

11. The statement that best describes the characteristics of "job shop" and "flow shop" manufacturing is:
    a. Job shops are generally used for smaller orders, while a high product output demand requires the organizational structure of a flow shop
    b. Flow shops are generally used for smaller orders, while a high product output demand requires the organizational structure of a job shop
    c. Flow shop manufacturing channels materials in random directions, while job shop process flow demands that processes be completed in a specific and rigid order
    d. Job shops are the perfect vehicle for delivering mass-market products, while flow shops fit the demand for small specialized batches of finished product

12. The best definition of "assemble-to-order stock" is that:
    a. Such stock is fully completed and maintained in large quantities for shipment to customers in high volumes
    b. It is high-priced, specialty stock sold to customers in smaller batches
    c. Such stock is maintained in a nearly finished condition, which can be modified in the last phase to suit the customer
    d. Such stock is in the final stages of manufacture but has been delivered to a warehouse

13. The best definition of a "make-to-stock" manufacturing order is that it:
    a. Is maintained in a nearly finished condition, which can be modified in the last phase to suit the customer
    b. Is for high-priced, specialty stock sold to customers in smaller batches
    c. Contains several versions of the same product, which is split into smaller batches for shipment
    d. Is competitively priced standard stock that can be shipped and inventoried in large quantities

14. A direct sales computer manufacturer advertises it can have a finished computer delivered according to your specifications within a short period of time. Such a manufacturer-seller would likely employ a
    a. Make-to-stock manufacturing strategy
    b. Make-to-assemble manufacturing strategy
    c. Make-to-order manufacturing strategy
    d. Combination strategy of all of the above methods

15. Inventory management is of the utmost importance to profitability because:
    a. Component supplies and raw materials are needed to sustain make-to-stock manufacturing
    b. It is the most expensive aspect of manufacturing
    c. It is a multifaceted activity wherein poor management can cause losses along all aspects of the manufacturing process, from project conception to completed product
    d. Transportation and storage costs are expensive

16. Define the term "nonconforming inventory."
    a. Nonconforming inventory is inventory in excess of customer order quantities and may be offered for sale by other departments
    b. Nonconforming inventory refers to inventory used only in job shops
    c. Nonconforming inventory is inventory that does not meet basic required specifications and therefore cannot be used in manufacture
    d. Nonconforming inventory is inventory that exceeds basic required specifications and is typically used in specialized batch runs of higher-priced finished products

17. Two common types of reordering strategies are:
    a. Centralized and decentralized reordering
    b. Time-based and inventory-level reordering
    c. Monthly and quarterly reordering
    d. Statistically based ordering and market research–based ordering

18. Inasmuch as insufficient capacity can cause bottlenecks as an oversupply of inventory is fed into a limited-capacity manufacturing process, the best potential remedy may be to:
    a. Increase capacity through alternate routing
    b. Subcontract
    c. Add personnel and new equipment
    d. All of the above

19. The process of adhering to the completed product and delivery date of the master production schedule and working back to the beginning point of manufacture is called
    a. MRP logic
    b. MPS logic
    c. Master production scheduling
    d. Supply chain management logic

20. At the end of every week, a manager inventories the number of widgets available for the following week's manufacturing to determine whether the supply meets the TIL (target inventory level) requirement. The manager sends an automated order to replenish to the pre-established TIL. The manager is using the:
    a. Order point system
    b. Weekly production scheduling system
    c. Periodic review system
    d. Master production scheduling system

21. In which phase of MPC (manufacturing planning control) does capacity testing occur?
    a. Top management planning
    b. Operations management planning
    c. Operations management execution
    d. Master production scheduling

22. The activity in the operations management planning phase that aligns maximum production, material, and labor capacity is termed
    a. RCCP
    b. MRP
    c. MPS
    d. Distribution planning

23. The best description of the purpose of order review methodology is that it
    a. Employs the ordering point system to determine inventory levels
    b. Establishes a system for determining what to order in the way of materials, when to order, how much to order, and when to schedule delivery
    c. Employs the periodic review system to determine inventory levels
    d. Incorporates both computerized and manual counts of inventory

24. A key difference between obsolete inventory and nonconforming inventory is:
    a. Nonconforming inventory is always attributable to loss
    b. Obsolete inventory can sometimes be used by reworking
    c. Obsolete-inventory costs can generally be refunded by the supplier
    d. Nonconforming inventory can sometimes be used by reworking

25. A typical reason that inventory materials become obsolete is:
    a. A formerly popular product loses market share
    b. The inventory does not meet specifications
    c. New technology forces changes in the manufacturing process
    d. The manufacturer has higher than average storage costs

26. Which of the following statements about job shops is FALSE?
    a. A job shop has flexibility
    b. Job shop manufacturing occurs in a series of steps that rarely vary
    c. Job shops depend on workers with varied job skills
    d. Job shops are typically not the best models of efficiency

27. A plant visitor touring a manufacturing plant observes two parts bins being used to supply workers in an assembly flow process. The plant is most likely using:
    a. An automatic point reordering system
    b. A time period reordering system
    c. A weekly ROP system
    d. A visual two-bin reordering system

28. The fixed order quantity lot-sizing technique operates on the basis of:
    a. Ordering the same amounts of material at varying periods of time
    b. Ordering specific amounts of materials at specific periods of time
    c. Ordering varying amounts of raw materials or components according to actual demand
    d. Ordering varying amounts of raw materials or components according to demand projections

29. Production planners communicate with floor operations supervisors in a variety of ways, but one key method is the:
    a. Daily inventory report
    b. Planning report
    c. Master planning schedule
    d. Daily dispatch

30. The chief elements represented in the EOQ formula for inventory are:
    a. Cost per item, cyclical demand, annual quantity ordered, and inventory holding cost
    b. Cost per item, setup cost, annual quantity ordered, inventory holding cost
    c. Setup cost, inventory holding cost, average lead time, and cyclical demand
    d. Annual quantity ordered, cost per item, inventory holding cost, averaged annual ROP

31. From the choices below, pick the statement that best describes the impact of larger orders on ordering/setup costs.
    a. Increasing order size increases ordering/setup costs
    b. Increasing order size tends to decrease ordering/setup costs
    c. Increasing order size has no effect upon ordering/setup costs
    d. Increasing order size increases carry costs but that is all

32. Among the factors a production supervisor should be familiar with are minimum, maximum, and multiple order quantities. The importance of these elements is that
   a. They impose restrictions upon ordering that must be recognized.
   b. They are used to set up the master planning schedule.
   c. They represent options for the production supervisor who must choose among them.
   d. All of the above

33. Inaccuracy in demand forecasting can be buffered by:
   a. Increasing or decreasing lot sizes
   b. Increasing the market research budget
   c. Maintaining safety stock
   d. Adhering rigidly to capacity limitations

34. Lot-based procurement refers to a type of supply acquisition that:
   a. Contracts for ongoing delivery of unfinished products for manufacture
   b. Represents a limited commitment to the supplier for a specific amount of qualified raw material or components
   c. Subcontracts a supplier to deliver materials needed for manufacture for a set length of time.
   d. Subcontracts suppliers to deliver materials according to demand cycles

35. Procurement supply scheduling is the preferred method of companies' _____.
   a. with an ongoing need of materials or components for manufacturing
   b. with a onetime limited need of specific lot-sized quantities of components or raw material
   c. that are not located near motor freight or rail freight terminals
   d. that contract middlemen to schedule and deliver materials for manufacturing

36. The process of intermittent manufacturing may be implemented for a manufacturing business that _____.
   a. manufactures standard batches of identical products
   b. needs to manufacture batches of the same product with the same specifications
   c. needs to manufacture batches of finished products that vary in terms of composition and family groupings
   d. has a single-path assembly process

37. A factory that manufactures a single product to a single set of specifications would most likely employ:
   a. An intermittent manufacturing process
   b. Manufacturing by lots or in batch production
   c. Continuous flow production
   d. All of the above processes

38. One advantage of setting up a continuous flow shop manufacturing a single product to the same specifications is that:
 a. Machinery work stations can be more easily located in a way that minimizes throughput time, inventory, and material handling
 b. It is very easy to manufacture a large, complex object through this process
 c. Alternative manufacturing methods can be employed
 d. The work may be redirected from a bottlenecked work station to one that is idle

39. JIT, or just-in-time, manufacturing means that:
 a. Raw materials and components can be used for project manufacturing as well as under flow line conditions
 b. Materials would ideally be delivered at precisely the time needed for manufacture and not allowed to build up in inventory
 c. Routing sheets are unnecessary
 d. The product(s) arrive at the customer's location on the specified date

40. "Lean manufacturing" incorporates many of the concepts of JIT manufacturing but adds additional elements like:
 a. Smaller inventories, faster deliveries from suppliers, and an adequate labor force
 b. Ensured efficiency of inventory flows through the manufacturing process
 c. Direct communication from workers on the shop floor to operations managers and suppliers
 d. Economies of scale and stable supplier relationships, combined with speedy communication through the supply line

41. Choose the best example of remanufacturing in relation to manufacturing:
 a. Auto engines may be remanufactured in a process in which a large number of engine parts are restored to Original Equipment Manufacturer specifications.
 b. Computers may be remanufactured in a process that replaces the hard drive.
 c. Auto radiators are commonly remanufactured and restored to original specifications.
 d. All of the above

42. Remanufacturing can have a deep impact on supply chain efficiency because:
 a. Component manufacturers do not like to sell components to remanufacturers
 b. Remanufactured products do not carry the same warranties or guarantees
 c. The needed materials or components are unknown until product disassembly in remanufacture, whereas the build schedule determines supply needs in new manufacture
 d. All of the above

43. The even balancing of an assembly line so that input from inventory is equal to output from production is called:
 a. Intermittent manufacturing
 b. JIT manufacturing
 c. Flow control manufacturing
 d. Synchronous manufacturing

44. The different methods of organizing inventory in limited access storage are:
    a. Dedicated, random, and zoned storage
    b. Factory, warehouse, and yard storage
    c. Point of use, point of access, and limited access storage
    d. Row, column, and line storage

45. The statement that best describes the difference between random and dedicated storage is:
    a. Random storage is reserved for high volume inventory; dedicated storage is favored for smaller batch runs
    b. In dedicated storage, parts and materials are always put in the same place; in random storage, materials are more frequently moved and handled so that they are near at hand
    c. Dedicated storage is bar coded but random storage is not
    d. Random storage relies upon RFID technology, but dedicated storage employs alphabetic systems

46. The statement that best describes the term "backflushing" is:
    a. The technique moves products backward through the assembly system.
    b. It refers to only liquid materials manufacture, which requires constant cleansing.
    c. The technique uses quantities of completed postproduction materials to streamline the inventory supply system.
    d. It is a preproduction process that streamlines inventory supply systems.

47. The difference between a hand pallet truck and a hand trolley is that
    a. Hand trolleys can be used to lift pallets in excess of 1,000 pounds, whereas hand pallet trucks cannot
    b. Hand trolleys can lift pallets, but only pallet trucks can fit through tighter aisles
    c. Hand pallet trucks are equipped with lifting hydraulics; hand trolleys are not
    d. Hand pallet trucks are motorized, whereas hand trolleys are not

48. Define the term "forward loading."
    a. Forward loading refers to a means of kitting materials so that the first used materials are placed in front stacks
    b. Forward loading refers to a means of stacking heavier freight or materials to the front of the trailer or supply bin
    c. Forward loading refers to the process of moving excess workloads to a future production run schedule
    d. Forward loading refers to the process of moving excess workloads to an earlier scheduled production run

49. Forward and backward loading are two options for:
    a. Storing raw materials and unfinished components
    b. Moving work that exceeds assembly and manufacture capacity to different fixed start times
    c. Transporting material to production flow lines
    d. All of the above

50. Flow control scheduling would be most advantageously used:
    a. In manufacturing processes where like machines are grouped in work centers
    b. In manufacturing processes where workloads must pass through a variety of work centers
    c. In manufacturing processes where customer orders are used as the basis of scheduling work production
    d. In manufacturing processes organized in straight-line assembly of high volume finished products

Answers and explanations

1. **B:** Answer choice "b" is the correct answer, and closer examination of the other answer choices should help you conclude those elements to be advantageous. Consignment stock is usually warehoused with a middleman in close proximity to the customer or directly within the customer's business. Carrying costs include cost of storage, pilferage, spoilage, insurance, and other handling charges. However, consignment stock helps to streamline the delivery process, maintains the relationship with the customer, and ensures that finished products or materials are ready for customer uses. The only "negative" is that the business providing the consignment stock must account for inventory carrying costs and ancillary charges.

2. **D:** The correct answer is "d," the production rate established to meet demand. The production rate set up by the management planning will impact the materials held in inventory and the ordering of resupply, as well as related activities, but the set rate of production is not a typical inventory function or cost. When managing inventory, however, the costs that may be categorized as inventory costs include the impact of stockouts, the cost of ordering and setup, "chasing costs," and the direct costs of inventory—insurance, spoilage, handling, insurance, etc.

3. **A:** The best answer is "a." Inventory is maintained in a condition ranging from single component parts to nearly finished product. Some companies may be in the business of adding the next step to the phase of processes that leads to a finished product. The amount of time it takes for that business to complete this process is called "lead time." The amount of lead time can vary, but it determines the amount of raw materials or unfinished product to be maintained in inventory. Carrying and transportation costs are relevant factors but should not be the primary factors in determining inventory.

4. **B:** The best answer is "b," though some of the other answer choices may have some relevance to the amount the accounting department will charge to inventory. The value of work in progress (WIP) consists of all carrying, production, and setup costs accrued before the product's or material's use in the next phase of production. Carrying and order setup costs are only part of the WIP value equation. The amount paid to the company providing the inventory is also a factor but does not include the costs of storage, handling, transporting, and maintaining the inventory.

5. **C:** The best answer is "c." The inventory management system must ensure against stockouts because they represent an expensive interruption of manufacturing and have a major impact on profitability. Aside from the idling of machinery and labor, stockouts may incur higher costs resulting from shipping back-ordered materials or products. Finding other suppliers is dependent upon whether the stockout is caused by the weakness of inventory management (ordering) or supplier inefficiencies. The fault most often lies with inventory management and ordering. Labor costs should never surprise because they are fixed, established costs, not likely to suddenly spike.

6. **D:** The best answer is "d." Setup costs are highest at the beginning of a manufacturing run. Once again, the other answers have some relevance to inventory costs, but with regard to

inspection and "chasing" costs, those costs accrue at all phases of the manufacturing process. "Chasing" costs are those costs associated with locating and moving materials held in inventory, and they are always a factor. Inspection costs apply whenever supplier materials are delivered, regardless of whether a product is at the beginning or the end of a production run. Answer choice "a" is simply wrong and misleading, as product lead times tend to be longer, not shorter, in the initial phase of production.

7. B: The correct answer, in this case, is the short answer shown in option "b." The reason the acronym APICS does not match with "Association of Operations Management" is that APICS sustained a name change. The original name of APICS was "American Production and Inventory Control Society"; however, its purpose is not to provide consulting services to the U.S. Labor Department. It does provide Certified in Production and Inventory Management (CPIM) certification. The basic goals for which APICS is organized are (1) to increase profitability through better inventory and supply chain management and (2) to ensure that managers have three related certifications, including CPIM.

8. C: The correct definition of the term "fluctuation inventory" is answer "c." Fluctuation inventory is sometimes referred to as "safety stock." It is used to compensate for unexpected surges in demand and to prevent customer stockouts. It is important to recognize that fluctuation inventory consists of finished product that can be immediately used. Pipeline inventory is product inventory in one of various stages of completion and cannot be used for stockouts or safety inventory for obvious reasons.

9. D: The correct answer is "d." Finished goods inventory is the combined fluctuation inventory and anticipation inventory. Both fluctuation and anticipation inventories are finished goods, but each has a different purpose. Fluctuation inventory is the amount of finished product made above and beyond the amounts required by a specific customer batch or order. It is sometimes called "safety inventory" because it is used to prevent stockouts and the resultant potential loss of market share. Anticipation inventory is the portion of finished product allotted to meet expected customer demand.

10. D: Answer "d" is the best choice. The relationship between materials planning and inventory can make a great difference to business profitability. Productive capacity must be modulated to fit with inventory supply. An overly optimistic production schedule, in which actual productive capacity is not able to keep pace with scheduling plans, will cause inefficient pipeline inventory buildup. The goal of lean manufacturing is to have the right amount of raw materials or partially finished inventory entering the next production phase. Accurate and consistent materials planning helps suppliers to manufacture, ship, provide materials and components as they are needed. Inventory buildups in storage or in pipeline bottlenecks add considerably to manufacturing costs.

11. A: Answer option "a" best explains the difference. Job shop and flow shop manufacturing fit the needs of different customers. Job shops are more loosely organized than flow shops, which house the processes of choice for large-scale manufacture of mass-market products. Job shops are flexible, and the work may move in a variety of directions, with different phases of production occurring in random order. The flexibility has certain advantages when small batches of finished product are the target objective. Flow shops are basically assembly-line operations that have preset sequences for the various phases of manufacturing a product.

12. C: Answer choice "c" is correct. Assemble-to-order stock is that which is maintained in a nearly finished condition, which can be modified in the last phase to suit the customer. The final manufacturing phase may be something as simple as color, as the customer determines that its retail business is selling many more red balls than blue ones. Assemble-to-order can be shipped with relatively short shipping lead times. Assemble-to-order is just one of three common manufacturing options; the other types are make-to-order and make-to-stock.

13. D: Answer "d" is correct. Keep in mind that the three types of manufacturing output orders refer to the product at the end of the manufacturing process, not the way the product is handled. Option "c" can be eliminated for that reason. Make-to-stock is the highest-volume type of manufacturing of products that can be shipped and held in inventory in large quantities. Such products are of a type routinely sold in large volumes, and so the manufacturing process takes advantages of economies of scale. It is the opposite of the relatively customized make-to-order and generally high priced stock.

14. C: The best answer is "c" because a make-to-order strategy is a method of producing customized output that is not intended to sit for long on store shelves. Computer configurations quickly become obsolete, so make-to-order takes advantage of lean manufacturing techniques to build a computer to the customer's specifications and ship it quickly and directly to the customer. A make-to-stock manufacturing strategy would negatively impact profitability because a large supply of computers would require steep discounting to get rid of inventory that runs the risk of rapid obsolescence.

15. C: Answer choice "c" is the best answer because it recognizes the multifaceted activity that can have multifaceted impact on the bottom line. Of course, there are elements of truth in the other answer choices, too, but inventory management consists of far more than transportation and storage costs and far more than component supplies and raw materials supplies. Inventory includes record keeping, inspection, spoilage, and location choices, among the myriad other elements essential to manufacturing profitability. Even elements like the cost of capital needed to purchase, store, and maintain inventory must be considered.

16. C: The correct answer is "c." Nonconforming inventory refers to inventory that does not meet basic quality specifications required for manufacturing. The nonconforming inventory may be internal or external. In the case of externally originated nonconforming inventory, a company may have the option of disposing of the materials or returning them to the supplier for a credit. In other cases, the materials may be reworked so that they meet specifications, but it is important to recognize that regeneration of nonconforming materials has costs that must be borne by the supplier or by the manufacturer.

17: B: The correct answer is "b," time-based and inventory-level ordering. Answer choice "c" mentions "monthly and quarterly reordering" but those are part of time-based reordering. Time-based ordering could just as easily be weekly or daily reordering, depending upon the type of manufacturing. Both centralized and decentralized reordering processes can make use of time-based reordering, but in the case of the decentralized process, inventory management can choose to distribute materials, components, or finished products according to either time-based or stock-level replenishment procedures.

18. D: The best answer is "d." All of the suggestions are ways typically employed when management needs to increase capacity. However, all of the potential remedies for insufficient capacity require a degree of foresight and planning. The spillover and inventory buildup caused by insufficient capacity can be costly as unfinished manufactured products pile up on the factory floor. Subcontracting, scheduling overtime hours, and adding new personnel and equipment cannot solve all problems and they are costly. Alternate routing is often the least expensive solution, but only when it does not create problems in other processes with other personnel.

19. A: The correct answer "a," MRP logic, i.e., materials requirements planning. It is important to understand how this works relative to the master production schedule, which has predetermined the amount of demand and the amount of production that will be required to meet demand. MRP logic requires that the production schedule be examined from end to beginning—a backstopping process and a process refinement that guarantees that the product will be manufactured and delivered to customers according to the sales contract. If some single element is insufficient or out of place, the problem is addressed before manufacturing begins. However, the main idea is to follow the sequence backward from end to beginning, with close scrutiny of all subprocesses.

20. C: The best answer is "c." The inventory management is employing the periodic review system. The availability of raw or unfinished materials needed for manufacture is reviewed according to an established time schedule. If there is insufficient supply to manufacture output according to the master production schedule, an order is placed to replenish the supply so that it conforms to the predetermined TIL or Target Inventory Level. Another and very different method often employed in inventory management is the "order point system," wherein orders are placed at irregular time intervals.

21. B: The best answer is "b." Capacity testing occurs at the operations management planning level. MPC, or manufacturing planning control, is one of three chief levels of MPC that are necessary to establish a successful manufacturing operation. Operations management planning includes scheduling for material requirements planning and sets the parameters for capacity requirements. It is at this point that the assembly systems are tested for capacity. If capacity is sufficient to process inventory levels and to produce output in accordance with the MPS, the final production plan is detailed by item number and date.

22. A: The correct answer is "a." RCCP stands for Rough-Cut Requirements Planning, an activity that tests the maximum levels of production, materials, and labor that the manufacturing system can sustain. The purpose of this type of planning is to even out and balance the production system so that bottlenecks do not occur and so that the amount of inventory being moved through the manufacturing phases neither overwhelms the system nor falls short of production targets.

23. B: The best answer is choice "b." The main objective of establishing an appropriate order review methodology is to determine how much inventory can move through the system capacity without causing bottlenecks or stockouts. Order review methodology may take advantage of various types of ordering systems, including both periodic review systems and ordering points systems, as well as hybridized systems. Order review methods can be computerized or manual, and the type utilized depends on the type of inventory and the inventory strategy a company uses.

24. D: Answer option "d" is correct in stating that nonconforming inventory can sometimes be used by reworking so that it meets specifications. In some cases, it is returned to the supplier for refund or credit. If the materials must be reworked, there are additional expenses that must be charged, usually to the supplier, unless otherwise specified. Obsolete inventory cannot be reworked. Nor is it spoilage. Unless obsolete inventory is sent accidentally by the supplier, it cannot be returned for a credit, and must be accounted for as a loss.

25. C: The best answer is "c." When new technology causes a change in the manufacturing process, stored or in-line inventory can become obsolete. The development of a new kind of fastening system, far less expensive than the one being used, could render obsolete the process and materials held in storage. In the case of "a," where a popular product loses market share and becomes unprofitable, the materials used in making the product are not necessarily obsolete, and may be used elsewhere. Inventory that "does not meet specifications" is termed nonconforming inventory.

26. B: The FALSE answer is the one shown in option "b." That description describes flow shops where manufacturing occurs in a series of steps that rarely vary. The purpose of a flow shop, and the reason for standardization, is to improve efficiency. A job shop is not a model of efficiency but depends on the abilities of its workers to apply a variety of processes to finish a product. Workers tend to be more skilled and may be assigned to various stages of the process. Continuous flow shops have little flexibility but they can produce the volumes required of mass-consumed products.

27. D: The correct answer is "d." The plant has implemented a visual two-bin reordering system. The bins are generally visually marked in some way with the ROP (reordering point). This type of system is inexpensive, requires no electronics to operate, and works very well in many situations. The reason for the second bin is to backstop the first, the one being used and depleted. A full bin represents the amount of raw material needed to produce sufficient product to meet demand, plus the appropriate amount of safety stock, during a specified lead time. When the workers empty the first bin and begin use of the second, the reserve bin is then replaced.

28. A: The correct answer is "a." Other terms for the fixed order quantity lot-sizing method of ordering are variable time method and fixed quantity method. The length of time between orders may vary but the lot sizes are always the same. The timing of order submission is typically based upon factors like the amount of inventory that can be cost-effectively held at the manufacturer or on the amount of inventory that can be delivered by the supplier. Aside from storage and production considerations, another method for determining when reorders are submitted is based on EOQ, or economic order quantity. The thing to keep in mind is that the size of the orders is always the same.

29. D: The correct answer is "d." Among the documents of high importance in communicating production data to manufacturing floor supervisors is the daily dispatch. The daily dispatch ensures that manufacturing sequences occur in a timely manner so that bottlenecks do not occur. The daily dispatch list shows the stop and start dates for each phase of manufacture and informs operations supervisors when work is due to arrive from other critical phases of manufacture. The dispatch list also prioritizes the inbound flow so that it can be assigned by shop supervisors.

30. B: The correct answer is "b." EOQ means economic order quantity and refers to the amount of materials supply needed to support a manufacturing plan. EOQ is also a mathematical formula derived from the following elements: setup cost, inventory holding cost, annual quantity ordered, and cost per item. The actual formula is EOQ=Sqrt (2US/IC., where EOQ is the fixed lot size, U is the annual quantity ordered, S is the ordering or setup cost, I is the inventory holding cost, and C is the cost per individual item.

31. B: The correct answer is "b." Ordering/setup costs tend to decrease with larger orders. However, ordering/setup costs are not the primary basis upon which order size is determined. Ordering/setup costs must be balanced against inventory carry costs and the output required. The EOQ, or economic order quantity, is a popular method of matching the quantities desired from the manufacture to the twin costs associated with inventory carry and ordering and setup.

32. A: The correct answer is "a." The factors of minimum, maximum, and multiple ordering quantities takes the theoretical order quantities and makes them fit the limitations caused by practical supply considerations. Since suppliers have costs that they must minimize to ensure profitability, they often set a minimum order quantity. By the same token, suppliers may have maximum order sizes that can be accommodated for reasons such as space, weight, and lead times. The manufacturer must adhere to these restrictions. An additional concern may be multiple order quantity, which relates to item grouping, such as would occur when products are produced as sets.

33. C: The correct answer is "c." It is important to recognize the importance of safety stock in manufacturing. Safety stock is the best buffer for inaccuracies in demand forecasting. The portion of the production output that is used to meet projected demand is called anticipation inventory; the portion of the finished goods inventory that remains unused is called fluctuation inventory or safety stock. The other answers are incorrect because capacity limitations do nothing in the way of predicting demand, nor will increasing or decreasing lot sizes. Increasing the market research budget does not guarantee accurate demand forecasting.

34. B: The correct answer is "b," and is evident in the term "lot based." Procurement refers to the process of acquiring materials need for manufacture and is usually done by the procurement manager on the basis of price, quality, and reliability of timely delivery. Lot-based procurement means that there is no ongoing commitment to the supplier after the purchase order contract is completed and the materials are delivered to specification.

35. A: Companies with an ongoing need of materials or components for manufacturing may choose to procure by a process of scheduling suppliers. The terms of scheduled deliveries are spelled out in the delivery contract. Total volume of material to be delivered under contract may be specified on a yearly basis or the contract may be open ended, that is, contracting the supplier to meet the manufacturer's production schedule. Prices are specified for the length of the contract and cannot be renegotiated until the contract expiration date.

36. C: The correct answer is "c." There are several different styles of manufacturing, and many companies need to be versatile in order to be successful. "Intermittent manufacturing" is the term used to describe an operation that moves batched lots of

materials or components through different paths and through different work centers. The output from intermittent manufacturing processes may result in different family groups of products, or a single product with variations in terms of color, finish, or other designations.

37. B: Choice "b" is the correct answer. The simplest kind of manufacturing process to set up is a batch production factory, sometimes referred to as manufacturing by lots. This is most likely the choice when the manufacturer wishes to make a single product to a single set of specifications. The manufacturer may have many different customers, but all customers want the same product, made to the same specifications. The opposite alternative is to employ an intermittent manufacturing process where products may take different directions and arrive at different work centers as they move to completion.

38. A: The best answer is "a." This type of solution to the single-product single-specification manufacturing cycle means that products can move predictably from raw materials to finished product. Everything about this type of process if predictable and single-product manufacturing reduces setup times. In continuous flow single line assembly, the work has only one path to follow. Choice "d" is undesirable and ignores materials handling and setup times and other logistical problems of manufacture. The key to single-product manufacturing is standardization—which increases profitability through shorter lead times.

39. B: Choice "b" is correct, since JIT, or just-in-time manufacturing, refers to process efficiency more than it does to the style of manufacturing process. Routing sheets may or may not be necessary, depending upon whether products take a single, standardized path or travel different lines and work centers, so answer "c" is incorrect. While answer option "d" is desirable, it is just not what JIT means. JIT is a technique designed to keep inventories at a minimum and to prevent bottlenecks by being flexible enough to adjust to changing demands upon production.

40. D: The best answer is "d," while more than one answer option may make limited sense. Lean manufacturing takes advantage of JIT processes in not overloading the production system with excess inventories. Lean manufacturing can readily adjust raw materials or components anywhere in the manufacturing process in order to prevent bottlenecks. A lean manufacturer make also take advantage of economies of scale that diminish inventory and setup costs, by stable relationships with suppliers that aid reliable communications.

41. A: The best example of remanufacturing is found in answer option "a." The remanufacturing process is generally occupied with expensive parts and components wherein the labor and reconstruction costs may be recouped and a profit margin added in. Auto radiators may be welded but are not complex enough to be a commonly remanufactured product; adding in transportation, handling, and other costs could supersede new manufacturing or refurbishing costs. A key factor of remanufacturing is that it replaces nearly all parts, and not just single components like hard drives. In repair, only the worn or broken parts are replaced.

42. C: Answer "c" is the correct choice. One of the largest difficulties posed by remanufacturing vs. manufacturing is the problem of supply, whether it is raw materials or component parts that are needed. The needed materials are an unknown factor until a damaged or worn product is disassembled and a process analyzer determines the number and types of parts or components that must be replaced. Naturally, this has an impact on

both inventory and suppliers. Remanufactured car engines carry guarantees similar to those of new engines, and suppliers would just as well sell to remanufacturers as they would to OEMs, or original equipment manufacturers, so those answers can be struck from the list of correct possibilities.

43. D: Choice "d" is the answer to this question. In synchronous manufacturing, a proper balance of workloads must be established as the work product moves through a variety of assembly and finishing stations. Supply schedules must be consistent with assembly line demand, and supply deliveries must be steady and reliable. Synchronized manufacturing can be enhanced by line side bin stocks, backflushing, and floor stock. This sort of kanban system can deliver supplies in the right quantities to balance output.

44. A: The correct answer is "a," and the phrase that provides a clue to the correct answer is "limited access" storage. Limited access storage also lends itself to "kitting." Answer "c" does mention three types of storage, but the question asks for three types of "limited access storage." The choice of a storage method should conform to the type of manufacturing being conducted. For example, limited access storage is more expensive and is generally reserved for higher-value products and materials.

45. B: The best answer is "b." By the process of dedicated storage, parts or materials needed for manufacture are stored in a place reserved for those parts and purposes. Random storage is a process that must be assiduously supervised so that materials can be properly sequenced into the production process. Efficient storage is a key component in keeping manufacturing costs down; an efficient storage strategy is one that is custom tailored to fit the type of manufacturing operation it supports.

46. C: The correct answer is "c." The term "backflushing" is a misnomer. The only thing that moves "backward" through the system is information. The information pertains to quantities of materials used in finished products at the end of manufacture—the postproduction environment. Through this information, the bill of materials may be corrected to reflect a streamlined inventory. Unlike the typical preproduction process for gauging inventory needs, backflushing provides a production control mechanism of greater accuracy and efficiency.

47. C: The best answer is "c," and it is important for inventory managers and materials handlers to be familiar with specifications and limitations of various types of moving equipment. Pallet trucks are equipped with lifting hydraulics with various lifting capacities, but one-ton pallet trucks are common. Pallet trucks and hand trolleys are used in tighter spaces where forklifts cannot maneuver. There are two- and four-wheel hand trolleys, with different weight capacities. Sometimes, motorized hand pallet trucks are used, typically battery and electrically operated.

48. C: The correct answer is "c." The thing to note is that loading, whether forward or backward, refers to the production scheduling. Forward loading is defined as the process of loading excess workloads to a forward scheduled period. Forward loading may be done when the load of materials and products moving downstream toward completion exceeds available capacity, as it often does. When the forward loading process detects overload, the excess work production and materials are shifted into a future scheduled production period.

49. B: The correct answer is "b." Both terms refer to options available when raw materials or components are moving through an assembly or flow line at a volume that exceeds capacity limits of the manufacturing system. The options are to move the excess to other fixed production schedules. In the case of forward loading, the excess workload is moved to a future production run schedule—a good choice if demand is currently being met. In the case of forward loading, the excess workload is moved to a future fixed production run schedule date. Backward loading moves the work to an earlier fixed start date.

50. D: Flow control scheduling is most often used in assembly-style manufacturing and a product can move along a set path. Efficiencies are created by mass production and overlapping workloads. Flow control scheduling should be supported by a plant physical design and layout. Machinery would be positioned in line rather than having all machines of the same type grouped together. Raw material or component inventory would be conveniently located to cut access times. Instead of manufacturing orders, schedules determine workflow and workload balancing.

Secret Key #1 – Time is Your Greatest Enemy

Success Strategy #1
Pace Yourself

Wear a watch to the CPIM Supply Chain Test. At the beginning of the test, check the time (or start a chronometer on your watch to count the minutes), and check the time after each passage or every few questions to make sure you are "on schedule."

If you are forced to speed up, do it efficiently. Usually one or more answer choices can be eliminated without too much difficulty. Above all, don't panic. Don't speed up and just begin guessing at random choices. By pacing yourself, and continually monitoring your progress against the clock or your watch, you will always know exactly how far ahead or behind you are with your available time. If you find that you are one minute behind on the test, don't skip one question without spending any time on it, just to catch back up. Spend perhaps 45 seconds on the question and after four questions, you will have caught back up more gradually. Once you catch back up, you can continue working each problem at your normal pace.

Furthermore, don't dwell on the problems that you were rushed on. If a problem was taking up too much time and you made a hurried guess, it must be difficult. The difficult questions are the ones you are most likely to miss anyway, so it isn't a big loss. It is better to end with more time than you need than to run out of time. You can always go back and work the problems that you skipped. If you have time left over, as you review the skipped questions, start at the earliest skipped question, spend at most another minute, and then move on to the next skipped question.

Lastly, sometimes it is beneficial to slow down if you are constantly getting ahead of time. You are always more likely to catch a careless mistake by working more slowly than quickly, and among very high-scoring test takers (those who are likely to have lots of time left over), careless errors affect the score more than mastery of material.

Secret Key #2 – Guessing is not Guesswork

You probably know that guessing is a good idea on the CPIM Supply Chain test- unlike other standardized tests, there is no penalty for getting a wrong answer. Even if you have no idea about a question, you still have a 20-25% chance of getting it right.

Most test takers do not understand the impact that proper guessing can have on their score. Unless you score extremely high, guessing will significantly contribute to your final score.

Monkeys Take the CPIM Supply Chain

What most test takers don't realize is that to insure that 20-25% chance, you have to guess randomly. If you put 20 monkeys in a room to take this test, assuming they answered once per question and behaved themselves, on average they would get 20-25% of the questions correct. Put 20 test takers in the room, and the average will be much lower among guessed questions. Why?

1. This test intentionally writes deceptive answer choices that "look" right. A test taker has no idea about a question, so picks the "best looking" answer, which is often wrong. The monkey has no idea what looks good and what doesn't, so will consistently be lucky about 20-25% of the time.
2. Test takers will eliminate answer choices from the guessing pool based on a hunch or intuition. Simple but correct answers often get excluded, leaving a 0% chance of being correct. The monkey has no clue, and often gets lucky with the best choice.

This is why the process of elimination endorsed by most test courses is flawed and detrimental to your performance- test takers don't guess, they make an ignorant stab in the dark that is usually worse than random.

Success Strategy #2

Let me introduce one of the most valuable ideas of this course- the $5 challenge:

You only mark your "best guess" if you are willing to bet $5 on it.

You only eliminate choices from guessing if you are willing to bet $5 on it.

Why $5? Five dollars is an amount of money that is small yet not insignificant, and can really add up fast (20 questions could cost you $100). Likewise, each answer choice on one question of the CPIM Supply Chain will have a small impact on your overall score, but it can really add up to a lot of points in the end.

The process of elimination IS valuable. The following shows your chance of guessing it right:

If you eliminate this many choices:	Chance of getting it correct
0	20%
1	25%
2	33%
3	50%
4	100%

However, if you accidentally eliminate the right answer or go on a hunch for an incorrect answer, your chances drop dramatically: to 0%. By guessing among all the answer choices, you are GUARANTEED to have a shot at the right answer.

That's why the $5 test is so valuable- if you give up the advantage and safety of a pure guess, it had better be worth the risk.

What we still haven't covered is how to be sure that whatever guess you make is truly random. Here's the easiest way:

Always pick the first answer choice among those remaining.

Such a technique means that you have decided, **before you see a single test question**, exactly how you are going to guess- and since the order of choices tells you nothing about which one is correct, this guessing technique is perfectly random.

Secret Key #3 – Practice Smarter, Not Harder

Many test takers delay the test preparation process because they dread the awful amounts of practice time they think necessary to succeed on the test. We have refined an effective method that will take you only a fraction of the time.

There are a number of "obstacles" in your way on the CPIM Supply Chain test. Among these are answering questions, finishing in time, and mastering test-taking strategies. All must be executed on the day of the test at peak performance, or your score will suffer. The CPIM Supply Chain is a mental marathon that has a large impact on your future.

Just like a marathon runner, it is important to work your way up to the full challenge. So first you just worry about questions, and then time, and finally strategy:

Success Strategy

1. Find a good source for practice tests.
2. If you are willing to make a larger time investment, consider using more than one study guide- often the different approaches of multiple authors will help you "get" difficult concepts.
3. Take a practice test with no time constraints, with all study helps "open book." Take your time with questions and focus on applying strategies.
4. Take a practice test with time constraints, with all guides "open book."
5. Take a final practice test with no open material and time limits

If you have time to take more practice tests, just repeat step 5. By gradually exposing yourself to the full rigors of the test environment, you will condition your mind to the stress of test day and maximize your success.

Secret Key #4 – Prepare, Don't Procrastinate

Let me state an obvious fact: if you take the CPIM Supply Chain exam three times, you will get three different scores. This is due to the way you feel on test day, the level of preparedness you have, and, despite CPIM Supply Chain exam's claims to the contrary, some tests WILL be easier for you than others.

Since your future depends so much on your score, you should maximize your chances of success. In order to maximize the likelihood of success, you've got to prepare in advance. This means taking practice tests and spending time learning the information and test taking strategies you will need to succeed.

Since you have to pay a registration fee each time you take the CPIM Supply Chain exam, don't take it as a "practice" test. Feel free to take sample tests on your own, but when you go to take the CPIM Supply Chain exam, be prepared, be focused, and do your best the first time!

Secret Key #5 – Test Yourself

Everyone knows that time is money. There is no need to spend too much of your time or too little of your time preparing for the CPIM Supply Chain exam. You should only spend as much of your precious time preparing as is necessary for you to pass it.

Success Strategy #5

Once you have taken a practice test under real conditions of time constraints, then you will know if you are ready for the test or not.

If you have scored extremely high the first time that you take the practice test, then there is not much point in spending countless hours studying. You are already there.

Benchmark your abilities by retaking practice tests and seeing how much you have improved. Once you score high enough to guarantee success, then you are ready.

If you have scored well below where you need, then knuckle down and begin studying in earnest. Check your improvement regularly through the use of practice tests under real conditions. Above all, don't worry, panic, or give up. The key is perseverance!

Then, when you go to take the CPIM Supply Chain exam, remain confident and remember how well you did on the practice tests. If you can score high enough on a practice test, then you can do the same on the real thing.

General Strategies

The most important thing you can do is to ignore your fears and jump into the test immediately- do not be overwhelmed by any strange-sounding terms. You have to jump into the test like jumping into a pool- all at once is the easiest way.

Make Predictions

As you read and understand the question, try to guess what the answer will be. Remember that several of the answer choices are wrong, and once you begin reading them, your mind will immediately become cluttered with answer choices designed to throw you off. Your mind is typically the most focused immediately after you have read the question and digested its contents. If you can, try to predict what the correct answer will be. You may be surprised at what you can predict.

Quickly scan the choices and see if your prediction is in the listed answer choices. If it is, then you can be quite confident that you have the right answer. It still won't hurt to check the other answer choices, but most of the time, you've got it!

Answer the Question

It may seem obvious to only pick answer choices that answer the question, but the test writers can create some excellent answer choices that are wrong. Don't pick an answer just because it sounds right, or you believe it to be true. It MUST answer the question. Once you've made your selection, always go back and check it against the question and make sure that you didn't misread the question, and the answer choice does answer the question posed.

Benchmark

After you read the first answer choice, decide if you think it sounds correct or not. If it doesn't, move on to the next answer choice. If it does, mentally mark that answer choice. This doesn't mean that you've definitely selected it as your answer choice, it just means that it's the best you've seen thus far. Go ahead and read the next choice. If the next choice is worse than the one you've already selected, keep going to the next answer choice. If the next choice is better than the choice you've already selected, mentally mark the new answer choice as your best guess.

The first answer choice that you select becomes your standard. Every other answer choice must be benchmarked against that standard. That choice is correct until proven otherwise by another answer choice beating it out. Once you've decided that no other answer choice seems as good, do one final check to ensure that your answer choice answers the question posed.

Valid Information

Don't discount any of the information provided in the question. Every piece of information may be necessary to determine the correct answer. None of the information in the question is there to throw you off (while the answer choices will certainly have information to throw you off). If two seemingly unrelated topics are discussed, don't ignore either. You can be confident there is a relationship, or it wouldn't be included in the question, and you are probably going to have to determine what is that relationship to find the answer.

Avoid "Fact Traps"

Don't get distracted by a choice that is factually true. Your search is for the answer that answers the question. Stay focused and don't fall for an answer that is true but incorrect. Always go back to the question and make sure you're choosing an answer that actually answers the question and is not just a true statement. An answer can be factually correct, but it MUST answer the question asked. Additionally, two answers can both be seemingly correct, so be sure to read all of the answer choices, and make sure that you get the one that BEST answers the question.

Milk the Question

Some of the questions may throw you completely off. They might deal with a subject you have not been exposed to, or one that you haven't reviewed in years. While your lack of knowledge about the subject will be a hindrance, the question itself can give you many clues that will help you find the correct answer. Read the question carefully and look for clues. Watch particularly for adjectives and nouns describing difficult terms or words that you don't recognize. Regardless of if you completely understand a word or not, replacing it with a synonym either provided or one you more familiar with may help you to understand what the questions are asking. Rather than wracking your mind about specific detailed information concerning a difficult term or word, try to use mental substitutes that are easier to understand.

The Trap of Familiarity

Don't just choose a word because you recognize it. On difficult questions, you may not recognize a number of words in the answer choices. The test writers don't put "make-believe" words on the test; so don't think that just because you only recognize all the words in one answer choice means that answer choice must be correct. If you only recognize words in one answer choice, then focus on that one. Is it correct? Try your best to determine if it is correct. If it is, that is great, but if it doesn't, eliminate it. Each word and answer choice you eliminate increases your chances of getting the question correct, even if you then have to guess among the unfamiliar choices.

Eliminate Answers

Eliminate choices as soon as you realize they are wrong. But be careful! Make sure you consider all of the possible answer choices. Just because one appears right, doesn't mean that the next one won't be even better! The test writers will usually put more than one good answer choice for every question, so read all of them. Don't worry if you are stuck between two that seem right. By getting down to just two remaining possible choices, your odds are now 50/50. Rather than wasting too much time, play the odds. You are guessing, but guessing wisely, because you've been able to knock out some of the answer choices that you know are wrong. If you are eliminating choices and realize that the last answer choice you are left with is also obviously wrong, don't panic. Start over and consider each choice again. There may easily be something that you missed the first time and will realize on the second pass.

Tough Questions

If you are stumped on a problem or it appears too hard or too difficult, don't waste time. Move on! Remember though, if you can quickly check for obviously incorrect answer choices, your chances of guessing correctly are greatly improved. Before you completely give up, at least try to knock out a couple of possible answers. Eliminate what you can and then guess at the remaining answer choices before moving on.

Brainstorm

If you get stuck on a difficult question, spend a few seconds quickly brainstorming. Run through the complete list of possible answer choices. Look at each choice and ask yourself, "Could this answer the question satisfactorily?" Go through each answer choice and consider it independently of the other. By systematically going through all possibilities, you may find something that you would otherwise overlook. Remember that when you get stuck, it's important to try to keep moving.

Read Carefully

Understand the problem. Read the question and answer choices carefully. Don't miss the question because you misread the terms. You have plenty of time to read each question thoroughly and make sure you understand what is being asked. Yet a happy medium must be attained, so don't waste too much time. You must read carefully, but efficiently.

Face Value

When in doubt, use common sense. Always accept the situation in the problem at face value. Don't read too much into it. These problems will not require you to make huge leaps of logic. The test writers aren't trying to throw you off with a cheap trick. If you have to go beyond creativity and make a leap of logic in order to have an answer choice answer the question, then you should look at the other answer choices. Don't overcomplicate the problem by creating theoretical relationships or explanations that will warp time or space. These are normal problems rooted in reality. It's just that the applicable relationship or explanation may not be readily apparent and you have to figure things out. Use your common sense to interpret anything that isn't clear.

Prefixes

If you're having trouble with a word in the question or answer choices, try dissecting it. Take advantage of every clue that the word might include. Prefixes and suffixes can be a huge help. Usually they allow you to determine a basic meaning. Pre- means before, post- means after, pro - is positive, de- is negative. From these prefixes and suffixes, you can get an idea of the general meaning of the word and try to put it into context. Beware though of any traps. Just because con is the opposite of pro, doesn't necessarily mean congress is the opposite of progress!

Hedge Phrases

Watch out for critical "hedge" phrases, such as likely, may, can, will often, sometimes, often, almost, mostly, usually, generally, rarely, sometimes. Question writers insert these hedge phrases to cover every possibility. Often an answer choice will be wrong simply because it leaves no room for exception. Avoid answer choices that have definitive words like "exactly," and "always".

Switchback Words

Stay alert for "switchbacks". These are the words and phrases frequently used to alert you to shifts in thought. The most common switchback word is "but". Others include although, however, nevertheless, on the other hand, even though, while, in spite of, despite, regardless of.

New Information

Correct answer choices will rarely have completely new information included. Answer choices typically are straightforward reflections of the material asked about and will directly relate to the question. If a new piece of information is included in an answer choice that doesn't even seem to relate to the topic being asked about, then that answer choice is likely incorrect. All of the information needed to answer the question is usually provided for you, and so you should not have to make guesses that are unsupported or choose answer choices that require unknown information that cannot be reasoned on its own.

Time Management

On technical questions, don't get lost on the technical terms. Don't spend too much time on any one question. If you don't know what a term means, then since you don't have a dictionary, odds are you aren't going to get much further. You should immediately recognize terms as whether or not you know them. If you don't, work with the other clues that you have, the other answer choices and terms provided, but don't waste too much time trying to figure out a difficult term.

Contextual Clues

Look for contextual clues. An answer can be right but not correct. The contextual clues will help you find the answer that is most right and is correct. Understand the context in which a phrase or statement is made. This will help you make important distinctions.

Don't Panic

Panicking will not answer any questions for you. Therefore, it isn't helpful. When you first see the question, if your mind goes blank, take a deep breath. Force yourself to mechanically go through the steps of solving the problem and using the strategies you've learned.

Pace Yourself

Don't get clock fever. It's easy to be overwhelmed when you're looking at a page full of questions, your mind is full of random thoughts and feeling confused, and the clock is ticking down faster than you would like. Calm down and maintain the pace that you have set for yourself. As long as you are on track by monitoring your pace, you are guaranteed to have enough time for yourself. When you get to the last few minutes of the test, it may seem like you won't have enough time left, but if you only have as many questions as you should have left at that point, then you're right on track!

Answer Selection

The best way to pick an answer choice is to eliminate all of those that are wrong, until only one is left and confirm that is the correct answer. Sometimes though, an answer choice may immediately look right. Be careful! Take a second to make sure that the other choices are not equally obvious. Don't make a hasty mistake. There are only two times that you should stop before checking other answers. First is when you are positive that the answer choice you have selected is correct. Second is when time is almost out and you have to make a quick guess!

Check Your Work

Since you will probably not know every term listed and the answer to every question, it is important that you get credit for the ones that you do know. Don't miss any questions through careless mistakes. If at all possible, try to take a second to look back over your answer selection and make sure you've selected the correct answer choice and haven't made a costly careless mistake (such as marking an answer choice that you didn't mean to mark). This quick double check should more than pay for itself in caught mistakes for the time it costs.

Beware of Directly Quoted Answers

Sometimes an answer choice will repeat word for word a portion of the question or reference section. However, beware of such exact duplication – it may be a trap! More than likely, the correct choice will paraphrase or summarize a point, rather than being exactly the same wording.

Slang

Scientific sounding answers are better than slang ones. An answer choice that begins "To compare the outcomes..." is much more likely to be correct than one that begins "Because some people insisted..."

Extreme Statements

Avoid wild answers that throw out highly controversial ideas that are proclaimed as established fact. An answer choice that states the "process should be used in certain situations, if…" is much more likely to be correct than one that states the "process should be discontinued completely." The first is a calm rational statement and doesn't even make a definitive, uncompromising stance, using a hedge word "if" to provide wiggle room, whereas the second choice is a radical idea and far more extreme.

Answer Choice Families

When you have two or more answer choices that are direct opposites or parallels, one of them is usually the correct answer. For instance, if one answer choice states "x increases" and another answer choice states "x decreases" or "y increases," then those two or three answer choices are very similar in construction and fall into the same family of answer choices. A family of answer choices is when two or three answer choices are very similar in construction, and yet often have a directly opposite meaning. Usually the correct answer choice will be in that family of answer choices. The "odd man out" or answer choice that doesn't seem to fit the parallel construction of the other answer choices is more likely to be incorrect.

Special Report: What Your Test Score Will Tell You About Your IQ

Did you know that most standardized tests correlate very strongly with IQ? In fact, your general intelligence is a better predictor of your success than any other factor, and most tests intentionally measure this trait to some degree to ensure that those selected by the test are truly qualified for the test's purposes.

Before we can delve into the relation between your test score and IQ, I will first have to explain what exactly is IQ. Here's the formula:

Your IQ = 100 + (Number of standard deviations below or above the average)*15

Now, let's define standard deviations by using an example. If we have 5 people with 5 different heights, then first we calculate the average. Let's say the average was 65 inches. The standard deviation is the "average distance" away from the average of each of the members. It is a direct measure of variability - if the 5 people included Jackie Chan and Shaquille O'Neal, obviously there's a lot more variability in that group than a group of 5 sisters who are all within 6 inches in height of each other. The standard deviation uses a number to characterize the average range of difference within a group.

A convenient feature of most groups is that they have a "normal" distribution- makes sense that most things would be normal, right? Without getting into a bunch of statistical mumbo-jumbo, you just need to know that if you know the average of the group and the standard deviation, you can successfully predict someone's percentile rank in the group.

Confused? Let me give you an example. If instead of 5 people's heights, we had 100 people, we could figure out their rank in height JUST by knowing the average, standard deviation, and their height. We wouldn't need to know each person's height and manually rank them, we could just predict their rank based on three numbers.

What this means is that you can take your PERCENTILE rank that is often given with your test and relate this to your RELATIVE IQ of people taking the test - that is, your IQ relative to the people taking the test. Obviously, there's no way to know your actual IQ because the people taking a standardized test are usually not very good samples of the general population- many of those with extremely low IQ's never achieve a level of success or competency necessary to complete a typical standardized test. In fact, professional psychologists who measure IQ actually have to use non-written tests that can fairly measure the IQ of those not able to complete a traditional test.

The bottom line is to not take your test score too seriously, but it is fun to compute your "relative IQ" among the people who took the test with you. I've done the calculations below. Just look up your percentile rank in the left and then you'll see your "relative IQ" for your test in the right hand column-

Percentile Rank	Your Relative IQ	Percentile Rank	Your Relative IQ
99	135	59	103
98	131	58	103
97	128	57	103
96	126	56	102
95	125	55	102
94	123	54	102
93	122	53	101
92	121	52	101
91	120	51	100
90	119	50	100
89	118	49	100
88	118	48	99
87	117	47	99
86	116	46	98
85	116	45	98
84	115	44	98
83	114	43	97
82	114	42	97
81	113	41	97
80	113	40	96
79	112	39	96
78	112	38	95
77	111	37	95
76	111	36	95
75	110	35	94
74	110	34	94
73	109	33	93
72	109	32	93
71	108	31	93
70	108	30	92
69	107	29	92
68	107	28	91
67	107	27	91
66	106	26	90
65	106	25	90
64	105	24	89
63	105	23	89
62	105	22	88
61	104	21	88
60	104	20	87

Special Report: Retaking the Test: What Are Your Chances at Improving Your Score?

After going through the experience of taking a major test, many test takers feel that once is enough. The test usually comes during a period of transition in the test taker's life, and taking the test is only one of a series of important events. With so many distractions and conflicting recommendations, it may be difficult for a test taker to rationally determine whether or not he should retake the test after viewing his scores.

The importance of the test usually only adds to the burden of the retake decision. However, don't be swayed by emotion. There a few simple questions that you can ask yourself to guide you as you try to determine whether a retake would improve your score:

1. What went wrong? Why wasn't your score what you expected?

Can you point to a single factor or problem that you feel caused the low score? Were you sick on test day? Was there an emotional upheaval in your life that caused a distraction? Were you late for the test or not able to use the full time allotment? If you can point to any of these specific, individual problems, then a retake should definitely be considered.

2. Is there enough time to improve?

Many problems that may show up in your score report may take a lot of time for improvement. A deficiency in a particular math skill may require weeks or months of tutoring and studying to improve. If you have enough time to improve an identified weakness, then a retake should definitely be considered.

3. How will additional scores be used? Will a score average, highest score, or most recent score be used?

Different test scores may be handled completely differently. If you've taken the test multiple times, sometimes your highest score is used, sometimes your average score is computed and used, and sometimes your most recent score is used. Make sure you understand what method will be used to evaluate your scores, and use that to help you determine whether a retake should be considered.

4. Are my practice test scores significantly higher than my actual test score?

If you have taken a lot of practice tests and are consistently scoring at a much higher level than your actual test score, then you should consider a retake. However, if you've taken five practice tests and only one of your scores was higher than your actual test score, or if your practice test scores were only slightly higher than your actual test score, then it is unlikely that you will significantly increase your score.

5. Do I need perfect scores or will I be able to live with this score? Will this score still allow me to follow my dreams?

What kind of score is acceptable to you? Is your current score "good enough?" Do you have to have a certain score in order to pursue the future of your dreams? If you won't be happy with your current score, and there's no way that you could live with it, then you should consider a retake. However, don't get your hopes up. If you are looking for significant improvement, that may or may not be possible. But if you won't be happy otherwise, it is at least worth the effort.

Remember that there are other considerations. To achieve your dream, it is likely that your grades may also be taken into account. A great test score is usually not the only thing necessary to succeed. Make sure that you aren't overemphasizing the importance of a high test score.

Furthermore, a retake does not always result in a higher score. Some test takers will score lower on a retake, rather than higher. One study shows that one-fourth of test takers will achieve a significant improvement in test score, while one-sixth of test takers will actually show a decrease. While this shows that most test takers will improve, the majority will only improve their scores a little and a retake may not be worth the test taker's effort.

Finally, if a test is taken only once and is considered in the added context of good grades on the part of a test taker, the person reviewing the grades and scores may be tempted to assume that the test taker just had a bad day while taking the test, and may discount the low test score in favor of the high grades. But if the test is retaken and the scores are approximately the same, then the validity of the low scores are only confirmed. Therefore, a retake could actually hurt a test taker by definitely bracketing a test taker's score ability to a limited range.

Special Report: Key Supply Chain Definitions

A

Actual Asset Life Maintenance Cost as % of Replacement Value: The process of identifying, prioritizing, and considering, as a whole with constituent parts, all sources of demand in the delivery of a product or service.

Actual-to-Theoretical Cycle Time: The process of identifying, prioritizing, and considering, as a whole with constituent parts, all sources of demand for a product or service in the supply chain.

Administrative Costs Associated with In-Transit Handling/Movement of In-Process Product: The process of identifying, prioritizing, and considering as a whole with constituent parts, all sources of demand in the creation of a product or service.

Asset Turns: The process of identifying, prioritizing, and considering as a whole with constituent parts, all requirements that must be satisfied by the supply chain execution.

Average days per Engineering Change: Courses of action over specified time periods that represent a projected appropriation of total supply-chain resources to meet total supply-chain demand requirements.

Average days per Schedule Change: The physical movement of materials (e.g., raw materials, fabricated components, manufactured subassemblies, required ingredients or intermediate formulations) from a stocking location (e.g., stockroom, a location on the production floor, a supplier) to a specific point of use location. Issuing material includes the corresponding system transaction. The bill of materials/routing information or recipe/production instructions will determine the materials to be issued to support the manufacturing operation(s).

Average Plant-Wide Salary: A record of specific information for each product, which defines the system parameters with which to effectively plan and execute using ERP (MRP, etc) systems.

Average Release Cycle of Changes: The series of task including placing product onto vehicles, generating the documentation necessary to meet internal, customer, and government needs, and sending the product to the customer.

Access Delivery Performance: The process of defining the requirement and monitoring the performance of the delivery of product to a customer. When physical delivery is out-sourced the performance is passed on to source for contract administration.

Align Supply Chain Unit Plan with Financial Plan: The process of revising the long-term supply chain capacity and resource plans, given the inputs from the strategic and business plans. This includes revision of aggregate forecast and projections related to supply chain, source, make, and delivery plans, as well as business assumptions.

Authorize Supplier Payment: The process of authorizing payments and paying suppliers for product or services. This process includes invoice collection, invoice matching and the issuance of checks.

Assess Supplier Performance: The process of measuring actual supplier performance against internal and/or external standards to develop and implement a course of action to achieve targeted supplier performance.

B

Build To Ship Cycle Time: The ongoing management of the activities associated with ensuring equipment and facilities are kept in proper order. This process element includes required repairs, alterations, calibration, and other miscellaneous items to maintain production capability of the manufacturing fixed asset base.

Balance Delivery Resources and Capabilities with Delivery Requirements: The process of developing a time-phased course of action that commits delivery resources to meet delivery requirements.

Balance Product Resources with Product Requirements: The process of developing a time-phased course of action that commits resources to meet requirements.

Balance Production Resources with Production Requirements: The process of developing a time-phased course of action that commits creation and operation resources to meet creation and operation requirements.

Balance Supply Chain Resources with Supply Chain Requirements: The process of developing a time-phased course of action that commits supply-chain resources to meet supply-chain requirements.

Bill of Materials (BOM): The Bill of Materials is a structured list of all the materials or parts needed to produce a particular finished product, assembly, subassembly, manufactured part, whether purchased or not..

Business Plan: A document resulting from a process of linking the long-range strategy with projections of revenue, activity, cost and profit. This process develops objectives usually accompanied by budgets, projected balance sheet, and a cash flow statement.

C

Capacity Utilization: A measure of how intensively a resource is being used to produce a good or service. Some factors that should be considered are internal manufacturing capacity, constraining processes, direct labor availability and key components/materials availability.

Cash-to-Cash Cycle Time: Cash-to-cash cycle time = inventory days of supply + days sales outstanding - average payment period for materials (time it takes for a dollar to flow back into a company after its been spent for raw materials). For services, this represents the time from the point where a company pays for the resources consumed in the performance of a service to the time that the company received payment from the customer for those services.

Commodity Management Profile: Number of distinct part numbers (purchased commodities) or service components/ resources sourced within the following areas: 200 miles, own country, own continent, and off - shore.

Complete Manufacture to Order Ready for Shipment Time: Includes pick/pack and prepare for shipment time, in calendar days.

Cost of compliance including administrative costs: Total MAKE cost to comply with regulatory requirements.

Cost of Goods Sold: The cost associated with buying raw materials and producing finished goods. This cost includes direct costs (labor, materials) and indirect costs (overhead).

Cost Of In-Process Product (WIP) Damaged from Handling/Storage as a Percentage of Total Material Cost: The costs of in-process product (WIP) damaged from handling/storage divided by the total cost of those materials.

Cost of Managing MAKE Information: The cost of managing, updating, and maintaining the information technology systems that support manufacturing operations.

Cost of Noncompliance: Measure of the MAKE costs for non-conformance with regulatory documentation and process standards set by external entities (e.g. government).

Cost per Invoice: All costs associated with the receipt, review, processing, and payment of a supplier's invoice for product received.

Costs Associated with Managing Production Performance as a % Manufacturing Controllable Cost: Ratio of Cost for Managing Production Performance to Manufacturing Controllable Cost.

Create Customer Order Costs: Includes costs for creating and pricing configurations to order and preparing order documents.

Cross training: The providing of training or experience in several different areas (e.g., training an employee on several machines rather than one). Cross - training provides backup workers in case the primary operator is unavailable.

Cumulative Source/Make Cycle Time: The cumulative external and internal lead-time to build shippable product (if you start with no inventory on-hand, no parts on-order, and no prior forecasts existing with suppliers), in calendar days.

Customer Invoicing/ Accounting Costs: Includes costs for invoicing, processing customer payments, and verifying customer satisfaction.

Customer Receipt of Order to Installation Complete: Includes product installation, acceptance and product up and running time, in calendar days.

Customer Signature/Authorization to Order Receipt Time: Time, in calendar days, from when the customer authorizes an order to the time that the order is received.

Capacity Constraints: A capacity constraint is said to exist when the available capacity at a resource may be insufficient to meet the workload necessary to support the desired throughput. A capacity constraint is often a bottleneck.

Consolidate Orders: The process of analyzing orders to determine the groupings that result in least cost/best service fulfillment and transportation.

Continuous Improvement Process: A process that identifies opportunities for performance improvement and facilitates their realization through the use of metrics, process development methodologies/approaches, project management principles, and reporting tools that support strategic and business plans.

Customer Replenish Signal: A requirement for product from a distribution location to a source location.

D

Days Sales Outstanding: 5 point annual average of gross accounts receivable ÷ (total gross annual sales ÷ 365)

DELIVER Cycle Time: All time associated with unloading, receiving, inspecting, and placing incoming materials into inventory and processing payment to the supplier including recording exceptions, moving incoming materials to storage location, and inputting data into inventory systems.

Delivery Performance to Customer Commit Date: The percentage of orders that are fulfilled on or before the original scheduled or committed date.

Delivery Performance to Customer Request Date: The percentage of orders that is delivered on the customer's requested date.

Demand/ Supply Planning Costs: The process of specifying, maintaining and dispositioning. Make's capital assets to operate the supply chain production processes. This includes repair, alteration, calibration and other miscellaneous items to maintain production capabilities.

Distribution Costs: Includes costs for warehouse space and management, finished goods receiving and stocking, processing shipments, picking and consolidating, selecting carrier, and staging products/systems.

Documentation: Number of orders without correct documentation supporting the order, including packing slips, bills of lading, invoices, etc.

Downside Delivery Flexibility: Percentage delivery reduction sustainable at 30 days prior to delivery with no inventory or cost penalties.

Downside Installation Flexibility: Percentage installation reduction sustainable at 30 days prior to installing with no inventory or cost penalties.

Downside Order Flexibility: Percentage order reduction sustainable at 30 days prior to shipping with no inventory or cost penalties.

Downside Production Flexibility: The percentage order reduction sustainable at 30 days prior to delivery with no inventory or cost penalties.

Downside Shipment Flexibility: Percentage shipment reduction sustainable at 30 days prior to shipping with no inventory or cost penalties.

Downtime in MAKE Due To Compliance Issues: The measure of process downtime due to noncompliance to external and internal regulatory documentation or process standards (e.g. specifications, SPC, governmental regulations, etc.)

Deliver Engineer-to-Order Product: The process of delivering product that is designed, manufactured, and assembled from a bill of materials, which includes one or more custom parts. Design will begin only after the receipt and validation of a firm customer order.

Deliver Make-to-Order Product: The process of delivering product that is manufactured, assembled or configured from standard parts or subassemblies. Manufacture, assembly or configuration will begin only after the receipt and validation of a firm customer order.

Deliver Stocked Product: The process of delivering product that is maintained in a finished goods state prior to the receipt of a firm customer order.

Delivery End Items: Products that have been acknowledged as received by the customer.

Delivery Plan: A plan for a course of action over specified time periods that involves a projected appropriation of supply resources to meet delivery requirements.

E

ECO (Engineering Change Order) Cycle Time: The total time required from request for change from customer, engineering, production or quality control to revise a blueprint or design released by engineering, and implement the change within the Make operation.

ECO cost: Costs incurred from revisions to a blueprint or design released by engineering to modify or correct a part. The request for the change can be from a customer or from production quality control or another department.

End-of-Life Inventory: Inventory on hand which will satisfy future demand for products that are no longer in production at your entity.

Equipment Utilization: Number of filled equipment SKU locations divided by the total SKU locations provided by the equipment expressed as a percentage

Equipment/Facility Maintenance Cost as % of Manufacturing Controllable Cost: Cost to repair, alter, calibrate and maintain production equipment divided by total Manufacturing Controllable Cost.

Enable Plan: A plan for the development and establishment of courses of action over specified time periods to appropriate delivery resources to meet projected delivery requirements. The plan contains necessary business requirements for information and relationships to effectively and efficiently PLAN the Supply Chain.

Establish Delivery Plans: The establishment of courses of action over specified time periods that represent a projected appropriation of supply resources to meet delivery requirements.

Establish Production Plans: The process that establishes courses of action over specified time periods to appropriate supply resources to meet projected production and operation plan requirements.

Establish Sourcing Plans: The establishment of courses of action over specified time periods that represent a projected appropriation of supply resources to meet sourcing plan requirements.

Establish Supply Chain Plans: Establishing time-based courses of action that attempt to appropriate and allocate supply resources to meet supply-chain plan requirements.

F

Field Finished Goods Inventory Days of Supply: The inventory which is kept at locations outside the four walls of the manufacturing plant, i.e. distribution center, warehouse.

Fill Rates: The percentage of ship-from-stock orders shipped within 24 hours of order receipt. For services, this metric is the proportion for services that are filled so that the service is completed within 24 hours

Finished Goods Inventory Carrying Costs: Sum of all costs associated with finished goods inventory: opportunity cost, shrinkage, insurance and taxes, total obsolescence, channel obsolescence and field sample obsolescence.

Finished Goods Inventory Days of Supply: Finished goods inventory days of supply are calculated as gross finished goods inventory ÷ (value of transfers/365 days).

Finished Goods Inventory Days of Supply: Plant finished goods inventory days of supply are calculated as gross plant finished goods inventory ÷ (value of transfers/365 days).

Forecast Accuracy: Forecast accuracy is calculated for products and/or families for markets/distribution channels, in unit measurement. Forecast Accuracy = Forecast Sum - Sum of Variance Forecast Sum Where: Forecast Sum = The sum of the units forecasted to be shipped in each month based upon the forecast generated at the critical time fence. Sum of Variances = The sum of the absolute values, at the forecasted line item level, of the differences between each month's forecast as defined above and actual demand for the same month.

Forecast Cycle: The time between forecast regenerations that reflect true changes in marketplace demand for deliverable end products. Only true "bottoms-up" forecasts are counted: for example, if weekly or monthly updates to the forecast only re-calendar or shift dates for the forecast to avoid changing the annual dollar-based forecast, they should not be considered true forecast regenerations.

Finalize Engineering: Engineering activities required after acceptance of order, but before product can be manufactured. May include generation and delivery of final drawings, specifications, formulas, part programs, etc. In general, the last step in the completion of any preliminary engineering work done as part of the quotation process.

Fixed Asset: Tangible property used in the operations of a business but not expected to be consumed or converted into cash in the ordinary course of events. Plant, machinery and equipment, furniture and fixtures, leasehold improvements comprise the fixed assets of most companies. They are normally represented on the balance sheet at their net depreciated value.

I

Incoming Material Quality: # Of received parts which fail inspection divided by the total # of parts received

Indirect to Direct Labor Headcount Ratio: Ratio of total number of employees required to support production in general without being related to a specific product, indirect labor, to the total number of employees that is specifically applied to the product being manufactured or used in the performance of the service, direct labor.

In-Process Failure Rates: The percentage of time work-in-process is not completed. 1 minus the percentage of completed work-in-process units.

Installation Costs: Includes costs for verifying site preparation, installing, certifying, and authorizing billing.

Intra-Manufacturing Re-Plan Cycle: Time between the acceptance of a regenerated forecast is by the end-product producing location and the reflection of the revised plan in the master production schedule of all the affected plants, excluding external vendors.

Inventory Accuracy: The absolute value of the sum of the variance between physical inventory and perpetual inventory

Inventory Aging: The percentage of total gross inventory (based on value) covered by expected demand within specific time buckets.

Inventory Cycle Counting Accuracy: The absolute value of the sum of the variance between physical inventory and perpetual inventory. Or the number of accurate part cycle counts divided by the total number of cycle counts performed expressed as a percentage.

Inventory Days Of Supply: Total gross value of inventory at standard cost before reserves for excess and obsolescence. Only includes inventory on company books, future liabilities should not be included. Five point annual average of the sum of all gross inventories (raw materials & WIP, plant FG, field FG, field samples, other) ÷ (COGS ÷ 365).

Inventory Obsolescence as a % of Total Inventory: The annual obsolete and scrap reserves taken for inventory obsolescence expressed as a percentage of annual average gross inventory value.

Item/Product/Grade Changeover Time: The time required for a specific machine, resource, work center, process, or line to convert from the production of the last good piece of item/product/grade of A to the first good piece of item/product/grade of B.

Identity, Assess, And Aggregate Delivery Resources and Capabilities: The process of identifying, evaluating, and considering, as in whole with constituent parts, all things that add value in the delivery of a product or services.

Identity, Assess, And Aggregate Product Resources: The process of identifying, evaluating, and considering, as in whole with constituent parts, all things that add value in the material and other resources of a product or services.

Identity, Assess, And Aggregate Production Resources: The process of identifying, evaluating, and considering, as a whole with constituent parts, all things that add value in the creation of a product or performance of a service.

Identity, Assess, And Aggregate Supply Chain Resources: The process of identifying, evaluating, and considering, as in whole with constituent parts, all things that add value in the supply chain of a product or services.

Identity, Assess, And Aggregate Delivery Requirements: The process of identifying, prioritizing, and considering, as a whole with constituent parts, all sources of demand in the delivery of a product or service.

Identity, Assess, And Aggregate Product Requirements: The process of identifying, prioritizing, and considering, as a whole with constituent parts, all sources of demand for a product or service in the supply chain.

Identity, Assess, And Aggregate Production Requirements: The process of identifying, prioritizing, and considering as a whole with constituent parts, all sources of demand in the creation of a product or service.

Identity, Assess, And Aggregate Supply Chain Requirements: The process of identifying, prioritizing, and considering as a whole with constituent parts, all requirements that must be satisfied by the supply chain execution.

Integrated Supply Chain (ISC) Plans: Courses of action over specified time periods that represent a projected appropriation of total supply-chain resources to meet total supply-chain demand requirements.

Issue Product: The physical movement of materials (e.g., raw materials, fabricated components, manufactured subassemblies, required ingredients or intermediate formulations) from a stocking location (e.g., stockroom, a location on the production floor, a supplier) to a specific point of use location. Issuing material includes the corresponding system transaction. The bill of materials/routing information or recipe/production instructions will determine the materials to be issued to support the manufacturing operation(s).

Item Master: A record of specific information for each product, which defines the system parameters with which to effectively plan and execute using ERP (MRP, etc) systems.

L

Load Vehicle, Generate Ship Documents & Ship: The series of task including placing product onto vehicles, generating the documentation necessary to meet internal, customer, and government needs, and sending the product to the customer.

M

Machine Wait Time: The percentage of time a machine facility is idle; 1 minus the utilization rate.

MAKE Cycle Time: The sum of the following average times: Order release to start actual build + Total build cycle + End build to leaves plant (i.e., moves to on/off-site distribution or goes to customer). For continuous and mixed processes, manufacturing cycle time is calculated as the average number of units (doses, kilos, pounds, gallons, etc.) in process divided by the average daily output in units.

Management Decision Timeframe Ratio: The ratio of the time needed to make a decision about a particular process divided by the cycle time of that process. (This generates a number that is better if it is lower). For example, if an operation can be performed in 2 hours, and it takes 4 hours to make a decision about that operation, the ratio would be 200%. The Timeframe would be affected by the time it takes to collect data, process information, develop knowledge and evaluate the situation, and implement the decision.

Manufacturing Controllable Cost: All costs under direct control of the MAKE function. These costs are: direct labor and expenses, indirect labor and expenses, asset charges, and excess material & packaging costs. (Raw and packaging materials used to make a finished good are not included.)

Material Requisition Cycle Time: The total amount of time required converting the identification of capacity needs for key material resources to the receipt of those resources.

Mean Time Between Failure: The average time interval between failures for repairable equipment and facilities for a defined unit of measure (e.g. operational hours, cycles, miles).

Mean Time to Repair Asset: The average time to repair equipment and facilities for a defined unit of measure (e.g. operational hours, cycles, miles).

Maintain Equipment / Facilities: The ongoing management of the activities associated with ensuring equipment and facilities are kept in proper order. This process element includes required repairs, alterations, calibration, and other miscellaneous items to maintain production capability of the manufacturing fixed asset base.

Maintain Source Data: The process of collecting information to support the day-to-day maintenance of all planning and execution data required supporting the sourcing process.

Make/Buy Decision: The output of the process used to determine whether a demand will be supplied with internal capacity or purchased through contract manufacturing and/or contracted services externally.

Make-to-Order - Discrete Manufacturing: The process of manufacturing distinct items, such as parts that retain their identity through the transformation process, that is intended to be completed after receipt of a customer order. Make-to-Order includes products built only in response to a customer order and products configured in response to a customer order.

Make-to-Order - Process Manufacturing: The process of manufacturing non-discrete products that have value added through mixing, separating, forming, and/or performing chemical reactions. Make-to-Order products are intended to be completed after receipt of a customer order. Then are built or configured only in response to a customer order.

Make-to-Stock: Production of distinct items, such as parts that retain their identity through the transformation process, that is intended to be shipped from finished goods or "off the shelf". Make-to-Stock products are completed prior to receipt of a customer order and are generally produced in accordance with a sales forecast.

Make-to-Stock - Discrete Manufacturing: The process of manufacturing distinct items, such as parts that retain their identity through the transformation process, that is intended to be shipped from finished goods or "off the shelf". Make-to-Stock products are completed prior to receipt of a customer order and are generally manufactured in accordance with a sales forecast.

Make-to-Stock - Process Manufacturing: The process of manufacturing non-discrete products that have value added through mixing, separating, forming, and/or performing chemical reactions. Make-to-Stock products are intended to be shipped from finished goods or "off the shelf," are completed prior to receipt of a customer order, and are generally produced in accordance with a sales forecast.

Manage Business Rules for PLAN Processes: The process of establishing, maintaining, and enforcing decision support criteria for Supply Chain Planning, which translate to rules for conducting business. Business rules align PLAN process performance measures with business strategy, goals, and objectives.

Manage Capital Assets: Acquisition, maintenance, and disposition of the capital assets. The process of acquiring, maintaining and dispositioning an organization's <capital assets> located at a supplier's facility and/or outside source, which are used to operate the supply chain.

Manage Channel Standards: The process of developing and maintaining customer and channel performance standards of an entire supply chain such as service levels, given service requirements by supply chain stakeholders/trading partners

Manage Customer Returns: The process of defining and maintaining the business rules, data, information systems, procedures, and transportation for the identification and disposition of customer product.

Manage Delivery Business Rules: The process of defining and maintaining rules which affect the acceptance of an order, based on quantity, method of delivery, credit, customer experience, etc. (Include distribution channel rules)

Manage Deliver Capital Assets: Acquisition, maintenance, and disposition of order management, warehouse and transportation capital assets. Determine material handling (inventory) pick pack & ship methods (inventory), and equipment.

Manage Deliver Information: The process of collecting, maintaining, and communicating information to support deliver planning and execution processes. The information to be managed includes: order data (customer preference, history, status, and delivery requirements, etc.), warehouse data, transportation data, deliver data.

Manage Finished Goods Inventories: The process of establishing and maintaining finished goods inventory limits or levels, replenishment models, ownership, product mix, stocking locations

Manage Import/ Export Requirements: The process of identifying and complying with import/export regulatory documentation and process standards set by external entities (e.g., government).

Manage Import/Export Requirements: The process of recording and maintaining regulations and rates that constrain the ordering and delivering of product. Determine customs requirements, establish letters of credit terms and conditions, etc.

Manage Incoming Product: The process of defining and maintaining the information that characterizes inbound logistics management of all supplier deliveries, including both physical and electronic goods and services. This includes carrier selection and management, tracking deliveries and import.

Manage In-Process Products (WIP): Management of the activities associated with handling / storage / movement of materials used to support production.

Manage Long-Term Supply Chain Planning: The process of establishing, measuring, and adjusting limits or levels of long-range supply chain capacity to meet long-range demand requirements, typically conducted at the business plan level. Key aspects of supply chain capacity include inventory, capital (fixed assets), outsource (contract manufacturing), and transportation.

Manage Make Equipment and Facilities: The process of specifying, maintaining and dispositioning. Make's capital assets to operate the supply chain production processes. This includes repair, alteration, calibration and other miscellaneous items to maintain production capabilities.

Manage Performance of Supply Chain: The process of measuring actual integrated Supply Chain performance against internal and/or external standards to develop and implement a course of action to achieve targeted performance. Performance targets established for the execution of supply chain processes are reflected in the process elements for PLAN, i.e. cost, delivery reliability, cycle time, responsiveness, and assets.

Manage PLAN Data Collection: The process of integrating and maintaining the accuracy of information necessary to balance supply resources to demand requirements at both the highest aggregate and lowest SKU planning levels.

Manage Planning Configuration: The process of defining and maintaining the information about a unique supply chain network for a group of similar or complimentary products through their full life cycle, including the evaluation of market need, product realization (development, introduction and production), product discontinuation, and after market support. This element also includes the management of critical sub processes needed to manage the life cycle of individual item numbers including item masters, routings, event planning (promotions, etc.), ABC classification, rationalization, and bill of materials.

Manage Product Inventory: The process of establishing and maintaining physical inventories and inventory information. This includes warehouse management, cycle counting, physical inventories and inventory reconciliation. For Services, this may include tracking the number of service providers and the financial resources committed at any given point in time.

Manage Production Data: The process of managing, collecting, maintaining, and communicating information to support MAKE planning and execution processes. The information to be managed includes production, order and process data.

Manage Production Data: Management, control, and dissemination of the information related to production processes required to manufacture specific products.

Manage Production Performance: The process of developing and maintaining performance standards and analysis methods to compare actual production performance against the established standards. This process allows the development and implementation of a course of action to achieve targeted performance.

Manage MAKE Regulatory Compliance: The process of identifying and complying with regulatory documentation and process standards for Make activities set by external entities (e.g. government)

Manage Production Rules: The process of establishing, maintaining, and enforcing rules for managing production details in line with business strategy, goals, and objectives. Production details include part/item master, bills of materials/formulas, routings, processes, equipment requirements, tooling, and other information specifying the method of production for a particular product.

Manage Sourcing Business Rules: The process of defining requirements and establishing, maintaining and enforcing decision support criteria, in line with business strategy, goals and objectives. The criteria translated into rules for conducting business within the enterprise and other legal entities including selection, negotiation, fulfillment, consideration and specific levels of collaboration.

Manage Supplier Agreements: The management of existing purchase orders or supplier contracts. This includes managing volume/step pricing, resolving issues, enforcing terms and conditions and maintaining an accurate status for existing purchase orders or contracts. Also, the management of a supplier certification process, which includes certifying new suppliers and maintaining the current status of existing suppliers.

Manage Supplier Network: The process of defining and maintaining a unique network of suppliers to deliver a specific product set. This includes establishment of a new supplier or maintaining an existing supplier and all the tasks and activities associated with identifying and qualifying the supplier and finalizing on the sourcing terms and conditions.

Manage Transportation: The process of 1) defining and maintaining the information which characterizes product, containerization, vehicle, route, terminals, regulations, rates/tariffs and backhaul opportunity (Characterization include information necessary to support maintenance of internal Outbound Transportation equipment - CAPITAL ASSETS) and 2) the management of transporters.

Material Availability: Availability of a product by location that is reserved, scheduled or available for sale.

N

Number of ECOs: Total number of revisions to a blueprint or design released by engineering to modify or correct a part, engineering change orders (ECO). The request for the change can be from a customer or from production quality control or another department.

Number of Supply Sources: Total number of internal and external direct production material suppliers used.

O

On Time in Full: Number of orders for which not all of the items on order are delivered in the quantities requested.

Order Consolidation Profile: Consolidation: is defined as the activities associated with filling a customer order by bringing together in one physical place all of the line items ordered by the customer. Some of these may come directly from the production line and others may be picked from stock. The following profiles have been captured: Shipped direct to customer's dock from point of manufacture (No Consolidation).Shipped direct to the customer with consolidation completed, local to customer by your transport company. Moved to on-site staging location for consolidation and shipment direct to customer. Moved to on-site stockroom for later pick, pack and ship. Shipped to different locations for consolidation or later pick, pack and ship.

Order Entry and Maintenance Costs: Includes costs for maintaining the customer database, credit check, accepting new orders and adding them to the order system as well as later order modifications.

Order Entry Complete to Order Ready for Shipment Time: Including release to manufacturing, order configuration verification, production scheduling, build, pick/pack, and prepare for shipment time, in calendar days.

Order Entry Complete to Start Manufacture Time: Time from completion of order entry to that of the release to manufacturing, in calendar days.

Order Fulfillment Costs: Includes costs for processing the order, allocating inventory, ordering from the internal or external supplier, scheduling the shipment, reporting order status and initiating shipment.

Order Fulfillment Cycle Time: The average actual lead times consistently achieved, from Customer Signature/ Authorization to Order Receipt, Order Receipt to Order Entry Complete, Order Entry Complete to Start-Build, Start Build to Order Ready for Shipment, Order Ready for Shipment to Customer Receipt of Order, and Customer Receipt of Order to Installation Complete.

Order Management Costs: The aggregation of the following cost elements (contained in this glossary):Create Customer Order Costs Order Entry and Maintenance Costs Contract/Program and Channel Management Costs Installation Planning Costs Order Fulfillment Costs Distribution Costs Transportation Costs Installation Costs Customer Invoicing/Accounting Costs

Order Management Cycle Time: The total amount of time required converting a customer order into a receipt by the customer.

Order Ready for Shipment to Customer Receipt of Order Time: The effectiveness of an organization in managing assets to support demand satisfaction. This includes the management of all assets: fixed and working capital.

Order Receipt to Order Entry Complete Time: Time required, in calendar days, for order revalidation, configuration check, credit check, and scheduling of received orders.

Overhead Cost: Costs incurred in the operation of a business that cannot be directly related to the individual products or services produced. These costs, such as light, heat, supervision, and maintenance, are grouped in several pools and distributed to units of product or service by some standard allocation method such as direct labor hours, direct labor dollars, or direct materials dollars.

Order Backlog: Orders that have been received and entered into the order processing system and are in a queue waiting to be processed and shipped.

Outsource Plan: A plan that describes how a company will utilize third party business partners to provide products and services which the company chooses not to provide with internal capacity. Outsource Plans can vary in detail from simple policy statements to highly detailed plans with specifics about the third party business partners, specifications for products and services, performance expectations, and contract considerations.

P

Package Cycle Time: The total time required to perform a series of activities that containerize completed products for storage or sale to end-users. (Within certain industries, packaging may include cleaning or sterilization.)

Packaging Cost: The cost to package product as a finished good, not including intermediate handling of materials, based on given number of Delivered Finished Goods.

Perfect Order Fulfillment: A "perfect order" is defined as an order that meets all of the following standards: Delivered complete; all items on order are delivered in the quantities requested Delivered on time to customer's request date, using your customer's definition of on-time delivery Documentation supporting the order including packing slips, bills of lading, invoices, etc., is complete and accurate Perfect condition: Faultlessly installed (as applicable), correct configuration, customer-ready, no damage

Plant Cost Per Hour: Total planning expenditures divided by the total number of hours spent exercising the plan

Plant-Level Order Management Costs: The aggregation of the following cost elements for which manufacturing is central focal point of orders (contained in this glossary):Create Customer Order Costs Order Entry and Maintenance Costs Contract/Program and Channel Management Costs Installation Planning Costs Order Fulfillment Costs Distribution Costs Transportation Costs Installation Costs Customer Invoicing/Accounting Costs

Product Acquisition Costs: Product acquisition costs include costs incurred for the production of product: sum of product management and planning, supplier quality engineering, inbound freight and duties, receiving and product storage, incoming inspection, product process engineering and tooling costs.

Product Losses (Sourced/in-process/finished): The total cost of lost material from receipt and inspection of raw materials to the shipping of the finished good, per given number of Inventory Turns or Delivered Finished Goods.

Product Management and Planning Costs as a % of Product Acquisition Costs: Product (Commodity) Management and Planning - All costs associated with supplier sourcing, contract negotiation and qualification and the preparation, placement, and tracking of a Purchase Order expressed as a percentage of product acquisition costs. This category includes all costs related to buyer/planners.

Product Process Engineering as a % of Product Acquisition Costs: Product Process Engineering - Cost associated with tasks required to document and communicate product specification, as well as reviews to improve the manufacturability of the purchased item expressed as a percentage of product acquisition costs.

Product Structure: Recipes / formulas / BOMs / that define the composition of a product

Product Structure Cycle Time: Total time from demand to release of product structure

Production Material Administrative Cost: Administrative costs associated with the handling / storage / movement of materials

Production Material Cycle Time: Time required moving material to point of use.

Production Material Handling Cost: Cost of handling/movement of materials used to support production.

Production Material Handling Damage: Cost of material damaged from handling / storage / movement as a percentage of total material cost.

Production Material Storage Cost: Cost of storage space used for the production materials.

Production Plan Adherence: Production Plan Adherence is calculated at the shippable end-product level in units, using the following formula: Production Plan - Sum of Variance Production Plan Where: Production Plan = The sum of the units planned to be completed (i.e., placed into inventory or shipped) in each month based upon the plan generated in the previous month. Sum of Variances = The sum of the absolute values, at the end item level, of the differences between each month's production plan as defined above and actual production for the same month.

Production Rules Preparation Cycle Time (PRPCT): Total Time from demand rules for production rules until releases of production details.

Published Delivery Cycle Time: The typical standard lead-time (after receipt of order) currently published to customers by the sales organization. For typical orders only, not standing/re-supply orders.

Published Delivery Lead Times: The typical standard lead-time (after receipt of order) currently published to customers by the sales organization. For typical orders only, not standing/re-supply orders.

Purchased Product by Geography: Number of the following distinct part numbers of: Raw materials, Externally manufactured intermediates, Toll manufactured finished products, Packaging product, Labeling product that are sourced within the following areas: 200 miles, Own country, Own continent, Off-shore.

Package: The series of activities that containerize completed products for storage or sale to end-users. Within certain industries, packaging may include cleaning or sterilization.

Pick (Staged) Product: The series of activities including retrieving orders to pick, determining inventory availability, building the pick wave, picking the product, recording the pick and delivering product to shipping performed in the distribution center in response to an order.

Plan & Build Loads: Transportation modes are selected and efficient loads are built.

Plan Deliver: The development and establishment of courses of action over specified time periods that represent a projected appropriation of supply resources to meet delivery requirements.

Plan Make: The development and establishment of courses of action over specified time periods that represent a projected appropriation of production resources to meet production requirements.

Plan Source: The development and establishment of courses of action over specified time periods that represent a projected appropriation of material resources to meet supply chain requirements.

Plan Supply Chain: The development and establishment of courses of action over specified time periods that represent a projected appropriation of supply chain resources to meet supply chain requirements for the longest time fence constraints of supply resources.

Planning Decision Policies: Any company policies that affect how a planning process is defined, approved, and performed.

Process Inquiry & Quote: Receive and respond to general customer inquiries and requests for quotes.

Produce and Test: The series of activities performed upon material to convert it from the raw or semi-finished state to a state of completion and greater value. The processes associated with the validation of product performance to ensure conformance to defined specifications and requirements.

Product: The end object of a transformation process that includes physical objects, information or services, "Result of activities or processes and may include service, hardware, processed materials, software or a combination thereof; can be tangible (e.g. assemblies of processed materials) or intangible (e.g. knowledge or concepts) or a combination thereof; can be either intended (e.g. offering to customers) or unintended (e.g. pollutant or unwanted effects)."

Product Routings: Product routings represent the way products are made and are integrated with the Bill of Materials. Key elements of proper Routings include proper sequence of operations, work center identification, relevant tolerances, run times, lot size and setups. The equivalent concepts for services are the workflow processes and rules.

Production Capacity: The total system-wide production ability to provide the maximum output of products or services.

Production Plans: A master production plan used to allocate capacity among manufacturing resources and schedule finite manufacturing activities or executing the performance of a service.

Projected Internal and External Capacity: An estimate of the amount of product or service a particular part of the business (internal capacity) or a third party business partner (external capacity) is capable of producing over a particular period of time when all factors that control the production processes are working optimally.

Q

Quarantine Time: Setting aside of items from availability for use or sale until all required quality tests have been performed and conformance certified.

R

Ratio Of Actual To Theoretical Cycle Time: The ratio of the measured time required for completion of a set of tasks divided by the sum of the time required to complete each task based on the rated efficiency of the machinery and labor operations.

Ratio of the Cost of Managing MAKE Information/Manufacturing Controllable Costs: The ratio of these two metrics provides an understanding into the effect of IT on the Make operating cost.

Raw Material & WIP Inventory Days of Supply: Raw material & WIP inventory days of supply are calculated as gross raw material and WIP inventory ÷ (value of transfers/365 days).

Raw Material or Product Days-of-Supply: Raw material or product inventory days of supply are calculated as gross raw material or product inventory ÷ (value of transfers/365 days).

Raw Material Shrinkage: The costs associated with breakage, pilferage, and deterioration of raw material inventories.

Receiving & product storage costs as a % of Product Acquisition Costs: Receiving and Product Storage - All costs associated with taking possession of and storing product. Includes warehouse space and management, product receiving and stocking, processing work orders, pricing, and internal product movement. This does not include incoming inspection.

Receiving and Put Away Cycle Time: The total amount of time required moving materials from an inbound location to an internal storage location.

Receiving costs as a % of Product Acquisition Costs: All costs associated with taking possession of product expressed as a percentage of product acquisition costs. This does not include inspection.

Receiving Cycle Time: Total elapsed time from time product is received to time it is passed to next process

Regulatory Documentation Cycle Time: The time required to complete regulatory documentation during a production run. The product cycle less this metric is the basic production cycle time. Does not include required product data collection for quality or process improvement.

Re-plan Cycle Time: The time between the initial creation of the regenerated forecast and its reflection in the Master Production Schedule of the end-product production facilities.

Responsiveness Lead Time: Minimizing elapsed time, including all delays, to receive a customer order and transform resources into goods and services, through to the point of customer receipt.

Return on Assets: A financial measure of the relative income-producing value of an asset. It is calculated as net income divided by total assets.

Rated Carrier Data: Contract rates and tariffs from carriers by commodity, lane, mode, etc. for shipments.

Receive Product: The activities such as receiving product, verifying, recording product receipt, determining put-away location, putting away and recording location that a company performs at its own warehouses. May include quality inspection.

Receive, Configure, Enter and Validate Order: Receive orders from the customer and enter them into a company's order processing system. Orders can be received through phone, fax, or through electronic media. Configure your product to the customer's specific needs, based on standard available parts or options. "Technically" examine order to ensure an orderable configuration and provide accurate price. Check the customer's credit.

Release Product to Deliver: Activities associated with post-production documentation, testing, or certification required prior to delivery of product to customer. Examples include assembly of batch records fir regulatory agencies, laboratory tests for potency or purity, creating certificate of analysis, and sign-off by the quality organization.

Reserve Inventory (Resources) & Determine Delivery Date: Inventory (both on hand and scheduled) is sourced and reserved for specific orders and delivery is committed to and scheduled.

Revised Aggregate Forecast and Projections: An update to the aggregate Supply-Chain Forecasts of Demand by Product Family supporting the Market/Channel Plans. Corresponding Projections, supporting Make, Source, Deliver, Inventory and Response Time Plans through the Supply-Chain are produced from these Forecasts Together, they represent balanced Supply and Demand.

Revised Business Assumptions: An update to the expected cause and effect statements that are the base for the Revised Aggregate Forecast and Projections. These are reviewed periodically with actual results to verify the linkage of actual cause and effect.

Revised Capital Plan: A revision to plan for capital expenditures necessitated by either changes in specific business plans or factors and assumptions affecting a business plan.

ROA: (See Return on Assets - Metrics)

Route Shipments: Loads are consolidated and routed by mode, lane, and location.

Routing Guide: Information used to select modes, transportation lanes, available carriers, etc. Listing or routes, carriers & rates.

S

Sales Per Employee: Total product revenue divided by total number of full-time equivalent employees

Schedule Achievement: The percentage of time that a plant achieves its production schedule. This calculation is based on the number of scheduled end-items or total volume for a specific period. Note: over-shipments do not make up for under-shipments.

Schedule Interval: This is the measure of the time required to regenerate the schedule to manufacture specific parts, products, or formulations in specified quantities within a specific time frame. The schedule interval must be less than the manufacturing cycle time to be

Scheduled Resource Cost: The measure of the cost of people, information systems, management direction, and any other costs associated with provided schedules for manufacturing.

Scrap expense: Expenses incurred from material falling outside of specifications and possessing characteristics that make rework impractical.

Shrinkage: The costs associated with breakage, pilferage, and deterioration of inventories.

SKU: Stock keeping unit

Source Cycle Time: Cumulative lead-time (total average combined inside-plant planning, supplier lead time [internal or external], receiving, handling, etc. from demand identification at the factory until the products are available in the production facility) required sourcing 95% (chosen to eliminate outlying data) of the dollar value of products from internal and external suppliers.

Source Flexibility: The time required to achieve a sustained increase in volume by 20%.

Source Identification Cycle Time: Total elapsed time from the time the requirement is identified until the source(s) are identified.

Source Qualification Cycle Time: Total elapsed time from time the source is identified until it is qualified and approved.

Source Selection Cycle Time: Total elapsed time from the time the RFQ is created until the contract is awarded and accepted by the supplier.

Sourced/In-Process Product Requisition Cycle Time: The time required to provide manufacturing with a needed component, service, or additive from the time of requisition to the time of delivery.

Sourcing Costs as a % of Product Acquisitions Costs: All costs associated with the identification of potential suppliers, evaluation of RFQ's and supplier qualifications and the generation of a contract expressed as a percentage of product acquisition costs.

Staging Time: The percentage of the time that the actual stage cycle time (interval of time required for individual products to move into a temporary holding location to the time of actual shipment or movement into finished goods) complies with customer requirements.

Storage Space Utilization: Volume of all materials stored divided by the total volume of the storage facility expressed as a percentage.

Supplier Cycle Time: The time required for a supplier to complete a single cycle, beginning with the receipt of an order and ending with the fulfillment of that order.

Supplier Fill Rate: The percentage of time a supplier completes a commitment to a customer to ship or deliver an order within 24 hours.

Supplier On-Time Delivery Performance: The percentage of orders that are fulfilled on or before the original customer requested date (suppliers performance measured by the customer).

Supply Chain Finance Costs: Costs associated with paying invoices, auditing physical counts, performing inventory accounting, and collecting accounts receivable. (Does not include customer invoicing/accounting costs.)

Schedule Production Activities: Given plans for the production of specific parts, products, or formulations in specified quantities and planned availability of required materials, the scheduling of the operations to be performed in accordance with these plans. Scheduling includes sequencing, and, depending on the factory layout, any standards for setup and run. In general, intermediate manufacturing activities are coordinated prior to the scheduling of the operations to be performed in producing a finished product.

Scheduled Receipts: Product due to arrive.

Select Carriers and Rate Shipments: Specific carriers are selected by lowest cost per route and shipments are rated and tendered.

Service Levels: Performance targets in service related measures (i.e. delivery performance, lead times, etc.) compared to the established service requirements. Service levels are established by balancing requirements against operational strategy.

Service Requirements: A set of minimum acceptable values that describe service requirements of a particular industry, channel, and/or customer segment.

Shipping Documents: Legal documentation of the contents of a shipment (e.g. way bill, bill of lading, export papers, etc....).

Source Plans: An aggregate material requirements plan used to schedule material deliveries to meet production plans.

Stage Product: The movement of packaged products into a temporary holding location to await movement to a finished goods location. Products that are made to order may remain in the holding location to await shipment per the associated customer order. The actual move transaction is part of the Deliver process.

Strategic Plan: A longer range, high-level plan that describes how a company intends to conduct business. Improve its market and competitive position, and increase its earnings performance.

Supply Chain Asset Management Efficiency: The effectiveness of an organization in managing assets to support demand satisfaction. This includes the management of all assets: fixed and working capital.

Supply Chain Costs: The costs associated with operating the supply chain.

Supply Chain Delivery Reliability: The performance of the supply chain in delivering: the correct product, to the correct place, at the correct time, in the correct condition and packaging, in the correct quantity, with the correct documentation, to the correct customer.

Supply Chain Flexibility: The agility of a supply chain in responding to marketplace changes to gain or maintain competitive advantage.

Supply Chain Performance Improvement Plan: A plan that describes goals and objectives for a supply chain and the steps that will be taken to reach those goals and objectives from the current performance levels.

Supply Chain Performance Metrics: Standard measures that indicate how well a supply chain performs within certain categories of performance known as Performance Attributes, e.g. delivery reliability, flexibility and responsiveness, cost, and asset management.

Supply Chain Responsiveness: The velocity at which a supply chain provides products to the customer.

T

Time and Cost related to Expediting the Sourcing Processes of Procurement, Delivery, Receiving and Transfer: Total time and/or cost variance to standard related to expediting a product through the Total Source Cycle.

Time and/or Cost Reduction related to Expediting the Transfer Process: Expediting cycle time for Transfer Process compared to the Standard Cycle time for the Transfer Process. Delta is the additive cost required by the disconnect.

Time and/or Cost reduction related to Source Identification: Desired State Source Identification Cycle metric compared to the As-Is State Source Identification Cycle metric. The delta being the cost /cycle improvement.

Time Interval Between a Performance Standard Request and Availability: The time interval from the receipt of a performance standard request and the availability of the standard.

Time to Comply with Regulatory Changes: Time interval between regulatory change issuance and implementation of the change.

Total Build Time: Total build time is the average time for build-to-stock or configure-to-order products from when production begins on the released work order until the build is completed and unit deemed shippable.

Total Deliver Costs: Costs associated with the Deliver Processes including execution, administration, and planning.

Total Internal and/or External Costs That Are The Result Of Inaccurate Production Rule Details: Direct and indirect costs that can be attributed to inaccurate production details. Includes rework, scrap, recalls, preparation, etc.

Total Source Cycle Time to Completion: Total elapsed time from time of requirement identification to time product is in the appropriate stocking location within the supply chain and the supplier payment is authorized.

Total Source Lead Time: Total source lead time is the cumulative lead time required to source 95% of the dollar value of materials from internal and external suppliers.

Total Supply Chain Costs: Costs associated with the supply chain including execution, administration, and planning.

Total WIP Inventory DOS: Total WIP inventory days of supply are calculated as gross WIP inventory ÷ (value of transfers/365 days).

Training/ Education: The total number of programs aimed at new work methods for experienced workers and short courses in current practices for new employees to increase productivity.

Transfer and Product Storage Costs as a % of Product Acquisition Costs: All costs associated with the storage and/or movement of the product to the next appropriate stocking location (transfer point) in the supply chain expressed as a percentage of product acquisition costs.

Transfer Cycle Time: Total elapsed time from the time the product is presented for transfer until product is moved to the next process.

Transportation Costs: Includes all company paid freight and duties from point of manufacture to end-customer or channel.

U

Unit Cost: Total labor, material, and overhead cost for one unit production, e.g., one part, one gallon, one pound.

Unplanned Maintenance Downtime % of total Production Time: Percent of time facilities or equipment are unavailable when scheduled compared to the Total Build Time (Production Time).

Upside Delivery Flexibility: Number of days required to achieve an unplanned sustainable 20% increase in deliveries.

Upside Installation Flexibility: Number of days required to achieve an unplanned sustainable 20% increase in installations

Upside Order Flexibility: Number of days required to achieve an unplanned sustainable 20% increase in orders.

Upside Production Flexibility: The number of days required to achieve an unplanned sustainable 20% increase in production.

Upside Shipment Flexibility: Number of days required to achieve an unplanned sustainable 20% increase in shipments.

V

Validation Frequency: The amount of time between reviews of a process. For example, Production Process Validation Frequency would refer to the amount of time between the reviews of the Production Process. This generally would be performed periodically to ensure that the process is generating the desired results with the desired inputs.

Value of assets provided by service provider (cost avoidance): Value of process and/or procedure provided by a service provider that directly results in cost savings in reviewing and selecting a source.

Value-Added Employee Productivity: Value added per employee is calculated as total product revenue less total material purchases ÷ total employment (in full-time equivalents).

Verification Costs as a % of Product Acquisition Costs: All costs associated with verifying the product meets all quality and contract specifications expressed as a percentage of product acquisition costs.

Verification Cycle Time: Total elapsed time from time product starts the validation process until it moves to the next process.

W

Warranty and Returns: Number of returns within the warranty period. Warranty is a commitment, either expressed or implied, that a certain fact regarding the subject matter of a contract is presently true or will be true.

Warranty Costs: Warranty costs include materials, labor and problem diagnosis for product defects.

Y

Yield: The ratio of usable output from a process to its input.

Yield Variability: The condition that occurs when the output of a process is not consistently repeatable either in quantity, quality, or combination of these.

Special Report: Additional Bonus Material

Due to our efforts to try to keep this book to a manageable length, we've created a link that will give you access to all of your additional bonus material.

Please visit http://www.mometrix.com/bonus948/cpimscm to access the information.